FASCINATING FUNGI OF NEW ENGLAND

By LAWRENCE MILLMAN

Foreword by GARY LINCOFF

Illustrated by RICK KOLLATH

T0161007

Kollath+Stensaas Publishing
394 Lake Avenue South, Suite 406
Duluth, MN 55802
Office: 218.727.1731
Orders: 800.678.7006
info@kollathstensaas.com
www.kollathstensaas.com

FASCINATING FUNGI *of* NEW ENGLAND

Printed in the United States of America.
10 9 8 7 6 5 4 3 2 1 First Edition

Graphic Designer, Illustrator: Rick Kollath with illustration assistance from Bonnie Wenborg and Danielle Rhodes
Editorial Director: Mark Sparky Stensaas

ISBN-13: 978-1-936571-01-7

Cover illustration shows a group of Wine-cap Stropharia mushrooms, Stropharia rugosoannulata.

ACKNOWLEDGEMENTS

It's impossible to be a mycologist and not receive mycological help. Among my helpmates, I'd like to single out Donald Pfister, Kathie Hodge, Leif Ryvarden and the late, great Sam Ristich for their expertise, not to mention their willingness to offer me huge chunks of their time. Other myco-minded individuals who've joined me on forays, provided me with IDs or simply supported my fungal habit include (in mostly alphabetical order): David Arora, Tim Baroni, Elizabeth Cherniak, Joe Choiniere, Matthew Delisle, Kay Fairweather, Jim Ginns, Susan Goldhor, Tonya Hauff, Jason Karakehian, Gary Lincoff, Jean Lodge, Deb Maestro, Barbara Millman, Maria Mitchell Association, the late Evgenia Model, Kate Mohatt, Monty Montgomery, Tom Murray, Bill Neill, Tuomo Niemela, Diane Pleninger, George Riner, Judy Roger, Jack Rogers, Antonio Sanchez, Elio Schaechter, Vlad Shalamov, Paul Stamets, Ernie Steinauer, Timo Vartiainen, Andrus Voitk, Tom Volk, Joseph Warfel, Elizabeth Wylde, the doctor on the *Orlova* and the Inuit in Kuujjuaq. *Fungi sint semper vobiscum, amicis!*

I'd like to thank the staff at Harvard's Farlow Herbarium, especially Gretchen Wade and Lisa Decesare, who always respond to my requests for obscure mycological tomes with unfailing good humor. Several of the descriptions in this book originally appeared in *Fascinating Fungi of the North Woods*, for which I'd also like to thank Larry Weber and Cora Mollen. Then there's Rick Kollath, the book's illustrator. His drawings are a splendid complement to my descriptions of fungi, much better than if I had managed to procure a world-class macrophotographer to take pictures of them. For good drawings can combine and/or highlight diagnostic features and/or field characteristics in a way that good photographs cannot. I tip my hat to you, Rick. And to Sparky Stensaas, who proves the dictum that he who edits least edits best, I tip my hat as well. Last but far from least, I'd like to express my gratitude to the myriad denizens of Kingdom Fungi, who never cease to amaze, confuse, humble and charm me.

Lawrence Millman

Cambridge, Massachusetts

June 2011

For Kathie,

dear friend, expert mycologist, and also expert photoshopper of skeletons

FOREWORD

New England has a long and distinguished history of publications in the natural sciences. No less an observer than Henry David Thoreau recorded every stage in the life cycle of nearly every plant he came across over years of daily rambles in New England. Nothing comparable exists for the mushrooms, alas, but we do now have a couple of generations of mycologists, both professional and amateur, who have been following the mushrooms as devotedly as fans follow the Red Sox. One of these, Walter Henry Snell, even changed careers from being a catcher for the 1913 Boston Red Sox to becoming a professor at Brown University, and eventually publishing the best guide to a much-cherished group of mushrooms, the boletes of Northeastern North America.

Now we have a field guide to some of the most conspicuous, most important, most fascinating, even bizarre, mushrooms of New England. Larry Millman makes available for the general public some of what we mushroom hunters and scientists have been observing, collecting and photographing from Maine to Connecticut, from sea-level to over 5,000 feet, year-round. There is even a section in this book on finding mushrooms in January!

This book could have been subtitled "Robert Frost's neighbors" because most of the mushrooms in this book can be found within a few miles of wherever you live in New England.

While some mushrooms are very particular about where they can grow, there are far more that occur within a stone's throw of downtown Boston.

In this book we can find the most dangerous mushrooms of New England, like the Destroying Angel and the Deadly Galerina, as well as the best edibles, like morels and chanterelles and king boletes (porcini). We can also find here the ones that glow in the dark like the Jack O'Lantern and Night Light. Perhaps there are no more fascinating fungi than the stinkhorns, many of which are shaped like objects abandoned after a fertility rite, and which can smell to high heaven. Larry skillfully incorporates both the most common and the oddest of these fungi into the work-a-day world of the nature in which we all find ourselves enmeshed.

The illustrations by Rick Kollath are excellent, and the organization of the book helps the user readily locate the mushrooms found by what they look like, whether with gills or without, and where they grow, whether on the ground or on wood. There are numerous sidebars, which are a must to read, because they contain some of the most fascinating information available about these mushrooms. This book is a reliable guide for hunting mushrooms in New England, opening for many the exotic wealth of a previously unseen world beneath your feet. To paraphrase Robert Frost, one could do worse than be a hunter of mushrooms.

Gary Lincoff
New York, New York
June 2011

CONTENTS

MUSHROOMS...WHAT ARE THEY?

"What supreme good fortune—we're both alive!"

—John Cage, on finding an unusual mushroom

What is a Mushroom?

Contrary to popular belief, mushrooms are not plants. They inhabit their own kingdom, Kingdom Fungi, primarily because of their dining habits. While plants make food from carbon dioxide and light with chlorophyll as a catalyst, mushrooms must get their nutrition from organic matter in their environment... just like a certain hominid. In fact, DNA studies indicate mushrooms are closer to our kingdom (the animal kingdom) than plants are. This means that if you eat a mushroom pizza, the mushrooms have more in common with you than the tomato sauce does. What's more, fungal cells are so similar to animal cells that a surprising amount of information about the basics of human life has been inferred from the study of yeasts.

The word mushroom usually refers to a fungus with a fleshy fruiting body, so yeasts are fungi, but they're not mushrooms. Likewise, molds, rusts, wilts, conks, mildews, crusts, blights and leaf spots—all members in good standing of Kingdom Fungi—aren't mushrooms, either. Do such distinctions matter? At least not in this book, whose purpose is at once to describe and celebrate organisms that bequeath an almost infinite amount of variety, color and mystery, not to mention occasional weirdness, to our increasingly beleaguered world.

Given how frequently we encounter gilled mushrooms, this book is divided into two simple categories: gilled and non-gilled species. Gilled mushrooms include *Amanitas*, supermarket button mushrooms, oyster mushrooms, so-called magic mushrooms and almost all of the LBJs (Little Brown Jobs) that pop overnight on your lawn. Non-gilled species include boletes, sac fungi, chanterelles, bracket fungi, earth tongues, jellies, morels and tooth fungi. You don't need to worry about the last of these—tooth fungi seldom if ever bite.

A Mixed Bag

A mushroom has one and only one purpose in life. That purpose is not to gratify your palate or delight your eye, much less to aid and abet biodiversity, but to make spores. For spores mean more mushrooms, which means more spores, which mean more mushrooms. To maximize spore production, mushrooms have evolved not only an umbrella-like shape, but also shapes that resemble calamari, dogs' noses and bird's nests as well as the virile organ of the human male.

Regardless of shape, most mushrooms have a vegetative part called a mycelium. Composed of tiny hairlike strings called hyphae, a mycelium is constantly probing its chosen substrate in search of nutrients. It's usually so small that you can't see it with the naked eye, but size doesn't matter in the fungal world. What matters is creative talent, and a mycelium must have that in spades, for it's responsible for creating mushrooms more or less from scratch. I'll talk about this subject later when I describe fungal sex.

A typical mushroom has a cap, gills or pores, and often but not always a stem. A ring (annulus) may or may not be present. This last structure has nothing to do with whether or not the mushroom is married. Rather, it's a remnant of the partial veil that covered the mushroom's gills in their infancy. A

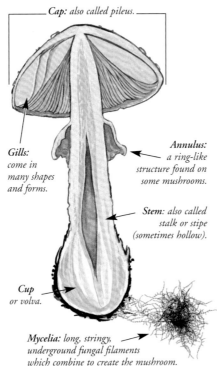

Cap: also called pileus.

Gills: come in many shapes and forms.

Annulus: a ring-like structure found on some mushrooms.

Stem: also called stalk or stipe (sometimes hollow).

Cup or volva.

Mycelia: long, stringy, underground fungal filaments which combine to create the mushroom.

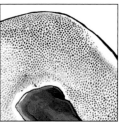

In place of gills some mushrooms have teeth or spines (left) or they have tubes with holes called pores (right).

ring may hug the stem or grasp it loosely, or it may even fall off, often leaving in its wake a so-called fibrillose zone. Another survival from a mushroom's past is the cup or volva that certain species have at the base of their stems. The presence of a cup will often help you identify a mushroom. Some *Amanitas*, for instance, are in their cups for their entire lives.

Under the cap of a gilled mushroom, there are (what else?) gills. Not to be confused with the breathing

COMMON MUSHROOM CAP SHAPES

Flat   Round   Bell-shaped   With Central Knob   Depressed   Conical   Vase-shaped

GILL ATTACHMENT

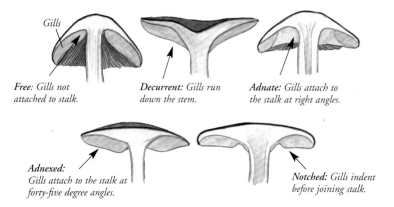

Gills

Free: Gills not attached to stalk.

Decurrent: Gills run down the stem.

Adnate: Gills attach to the stalk at right angles.

Adnexed: Gills attach to the stalk at forty-five degree angles.

Notched: Gills indent before joining stalk.

TYPES OF GILLS

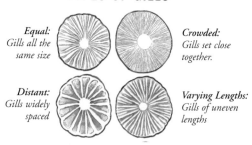

Equal: Gills all the same size

Crowded: Gills set close together.

Distant: Gills widely spaced

Varying Lengths: Gills of uneven lengths

apparatus of a fish, a mushroom's gills are adorned with thousands of club-shaped structures called basidia. These basidia are responsible for the production of spores. Since a stay-at-home spore is a useless spore, a basidium will forcibly eject its spores via a droplet of fluid combined with a sudden gravitational shift. The speed of the initial spore launch would put a marathon runner, not to mention a NASA missile, to shame.

After you've discovered that a mushroom has gills, don't get too smug. For you still need to determine in what way those gills are attached to the stem or indeed if they're attached to the stem. Not only that, but you also need to determine if those gills are widely spaced or bunched closely together. The accompanying illustrations will help you with those tasks. Actually, I shouldn't use the word task. For identifying mushrooms is a lot more fun than most activities in life.

A Mushroom's Life Cycle

There are spores everywhere. Literally everywhere. Perhaps half a million of these tiny seedlike propagules are currently occupying the pillow where you'll rest your head tonight. Likewise, an ordinary-sized puffball may produce billions of spores during its lifetime. But few if any of the puffball's spores or the spores on your pillow will ever grow up to become mushrooms. Such wastefulness is not uncommon in nature. Consider the number of unsuccessful sperm cells manufactured by the human male...

Actually, spores don't grow up. Under favorable conditions (sufficient moisture and the right nutrients), they form hyphae, then a mycelium. Ever probing the world for nutrients, a mycelium will eat anything that's organic. During an autopsy, I once saw a human brain (yum!) being snacked upon by the mycelium of an *Aspergillus*

MATURITY OF A TYPICAL MUSHROOM

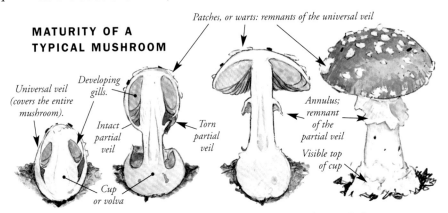

Patches, or warts: remnants of the universal veil

Developing gills.

Universal veil (covers the entire mushroom).

Intact partial veil

Torn partial veil

Cup or volva

Annulus; remnant of the partial veil

Visible top of cup

Emerging button stage

Mature fruiting body

species. Another fungus, *Geotrichum candidum*, reputedly eats CDs, but I suspect that it's really eating (yum again!) the bacteria on the CDs.

And now for some sex. Try to imagine the fungal equivalent of a singles bar. Two horny mycelia of the same species walk in the door. They do not exchange pleasantries or talk about previous relationships (neither, in fact, has had a previous relationship). No, they try to mate the moment they encounter each other. Most of the time they aren't successful because they're of different genders or mating types. In other words, they're incompatible. But if the

mycelia do succeed in uniting, maybe, just maybe the result will be (drinks on the house!) a mushroom.

Here I should mention that some fungal species have no interest in sex. Instead, they produce spores that are wholly capable of developing on their own. Such species are known as "imperfect fungi," although I suspect that they might regard their sexually licentious brethren as being the imperfect ones.

Basidiomycetes versus Ascomycetes

If a mushroom has club-shaped basidia, then it's called a basidiomycete. Chances

are, the next mushroom you see—whether you see it in the woods or on your front lawn—will be a basidiomycete. But what if that mushroom doesn't have basidia? What if it doesn't have gills, teeth, pores or even a cap? What if it isn't fleshy, woody, gelatinous or powdery, either? Could it perhaps be a species unknown to science?

Not likely. The mushroom in question is probably an ascomycete, so named because its spore-producing cells are called asci. In each ascus, there are usually eight spores lined up in a row like peas in a pod. Whereas a basidiomycete tends to drop its spores, an ascomycete tends to thrust them upward, although only for a couple of inches. Quite a number of ascomycetes are imperfect fungi (see previous section).

If a mushroom looks like a tea-cup, a saucer, a blackened tongue, miniature antlers, rabbit ears or a funeral urn, then it's probably an ascomycete. Morels are ascomycetes. So are Dead Man's Fingers. So are most yeasts. So, too, is the *Penicillium* mold from which Dr. Alexander Fleming derived penicillin. Indeed, some of the most diverse as well as most valuable fungi in the

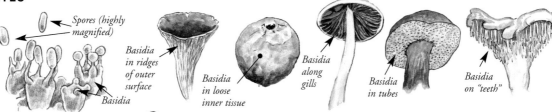

BASIDIOMYCETES

Spores develop on club-shaped basidia.

Spores (highly magnified)

Fleshy fungi break down into two groups based on how their spores are produced.

Basidia

Basidia in ridges of outer surface

Basidia in loose inner tissue

Basidia along gills

Basidia in tubes

Basidia on "teeth"

ASCOMYCETES

Spores develop in tube-shaped asci.

Spores (highly magnified)

Ascus

Asci on inner surface

Asci in pits

world are — to use the common mycological abbreviation — ascos.

Slime Molds

After a heavy rain, you might sometimes see what looks like dog vomit, scrambled eggs or tiny pretzels on a log or on the ground. Unless a sick dog or a disoriented short order cook has been in the area, you're probably seeing a slime mold or Myxomycete, not a fungus. Slime molds are members of the same kingdom as protozoa,

plankton and the parasites responsible for malaria — Kingdom Protista. Even so, they're often included in mushroom books because many of them look like mushrooms. But some of them

would seem to look like nothing else on the planet. A woman in Texas once saw a large fruiting of Scrambled Egg Slime *(Fuligo septica)* on her front lawn and immediately called the police, saying that extraterrestrials had landed on her property. The last section of this book has a representative sampling of slime molds, including the very species the woman in Texas mistook for an extraterrestrial.

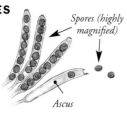

Fuligo septica

Eaters of the Dead

To survive, a fungus depends on organic material in its environment, but that material doesn't need to be living. Saprobes feed on dead or dying plant tissue, animal remains or that old carpet that's been sitting in your basement for years. Their hyphae release enzymes that break down the cellular structure of their host into easily digestible carbohydrates, proteins and lipids. Most of the time these enzymes can't digest healthy tissue.

Let's briefly segue to *Homo sapiens*, the species to which so many readers of this book belong. A healthy person is unlikely to get a fungal infection, but a person with a compromised immune system—i.e., someone weakened by AIDS, cancer or immunosuppressant drugs—is an easy candidate for such infections. A fungus regards an unhealthy person in much the same way it regards bioengineered wheat, a monoculture plantation or an injured tree... as food.

Saprobic fungi perform a valuable ecological service in New England. By recycling wood, they not only enrich the soil, but they also help create that soil. For the region still hasn't recovered from the scouring it received from Ice Age glaciers 10,000 or so years ago, and thus its topsoil is very shallow compared to, say, the topsoil of the Midwest. Thanks in part to saprobic fungi, that topsoil is now slowly returning to its pre-glacial luxuriance.

Saprobic mushrooms obtain nutrients by using enzymes to break down dead and decaying plant matter.

Loving Partners

Many fungi have evolved with vascular plants and trees, creating what's known as a mycorrhizal relationship. In such relationships, a mycelium forms a sheath of hyphae around a host's roots; this sheath, known as a Hartig net, helps that host absorb phosphorus, inorganic nitrogen, various micronutrients and moisture. In return, the host passes on 18 to 20 percent of the sugars created during photosynthesis to its fungal partner or mycobiont. Without these sugars, that partner would be in difficult straits, while trees or plants deprived of their mycobionts have been known to sicken and die. In effect, the fungus is an extension of its host's root system.

As with many relationships, sometimes a partner will cheat. Usually, the cheater is the fungus, and when the host learns about this, it's goodbye to your carbs, sweetheart. Sometimes, too, a third party like garlic mustard might damage the relationship. This

SYMBIOTIC MUSHROOM/TREE RELATIONSHIP

A mycelium takes carbohydrates from the tree's roots in exchange for nutrients the tree itself can't get.

The mushroom is only the fruiting body of the main part of the organism – the mycelium.

Tree roots

biennial herb from Europe releases an antifungal chemical in the soil that prevents both the fungus and its host from performing their mutualistic duties. Most states in the Eastern U.S. now have this noxious invasive, and efforts to eradicate it have thus far proved unsuccessful.

Many mycorrhizal species are so host specific that fungal foragers often don't look for the species, they look for the host. For example, Matsutakes grow almost exclusively with eastern hemlock in New England, while most *Suillus* species grow only with white pine. But you shouldn't assume the tree will be directly overhead. For a mycelium knows only about a tree's root system, not about its towering growth, which means it might produce a mushroom a hundred feet or more away from the actual tree.

Unloving Partners

In a bad marriage, one partner can make life miserable for the other. So it is with parasitic fungi. They're symbionts no less than mycorrhizal fungi, but they're usually not very nice to their hosts. Think sudden oak death,

wheat rust, Dutch elm disease and chestnut blight. Think *Herpomyces stylopage*, a fungus with such a specialized diet that it can only digest the sensory hairs on a cockroach's antennae.

In New England, not too many actual mushrooms are parasites. Those that are include the Honey Mushroom, some ascos, a bolete that attacks a puffball *(Boletus parasiticus)*, *Cordyceps* species that grow on insect larvae and underground truffles, the Powder Cap, *Hypomyces* species and certain polypores. Honey Mushrooms can be particularly vigorous in their assaults on healthy trees, but they can be saprobes, too.

If a human marriage is bad, one partner can divorce the other. Not so with fungi: a bolete that's parasitized by a *Hypomyces* can't get rid of that *Hypomyces* by divorcing it. Nor can the bolete take out a restraining order against the *Hypomyces*. This is too bad for the bolete, but not for the *Hypomyces*, which, if it could talk, might say, Hey, we parasites gotta live, too...

Collecting Mushrooms: The Basics

Many mushrooms elude field identification, so you may need to bring them

Parasites live off a host plant, endangering the host's health as it grows. The tree may eventually die but in the process create new habitats for many other organisms.

home for further study. There's no reason to feel guilty about this, since collecting a few mushrooms no more damages the fungal organism than picking fruit damages a fruit tree. But take only a few samples of each species, and be sure to fill up any holes or ruts you've made. If you happen to collect a species that you decide not to bring home with you, put it in the branch of a tree so that it can still drop its spores.

When I'm foraging for mushrooms, I always have an old Maine potato picker's basket strapped to my back, but any picnic basket, bucket, tub or large paper bag will do as a temporary home for your specimens. Also, put each mushroom in waxed paper or a small paper bag (but never a plastic bag!) with a slip of paper on which you've written the location where you found it, its color when fresh, the type of tree with which or on which it seemed to be growing and any unusual features (sticky? hairy? stinky? polka dots on cap?) it possesses. Certain features will not be visible to the naked eye, especially as that eye gets older, so you should always carry a 10x or 15x hand lens. A knife is also useful if you want to remove wood-inhabiting species from their substrate.

A friend of mine once got lost in the woods for almost two days while looking for mushrooms. He had neither a compass, a GPS or a map with him. To avoid suffering a similar fate, you should bring along at least a compass on your trips into the woods, especially if you're by yourself. If you're with fellow foragers, you may wish to bring along a whistle, too. Its high-pitched sound will alert your com-

panions to your whereabouts... or to the whereabouts of a patch of *Boletus edulis* too large for one person however greedy or voracious he or she might be.

A Very Short Course in Mushroom Identification

In trying to identify a mushroom, sometimes you'll win, and sometimes the mushroom will win. You can aid your cause by focusing on diagnostic features like the ones I mentioned in the previous paragraph. You might also smell a mushroom. One species I know smells like coconuts, and another one I know smells like marzipan. Certain boletes bruise blue-green or cinnamon-brown, while others don't bruise at all.

Is there (I'm not making this up) a nipple on the cap? A sharp or blunt nipple? Does the species grow in huge clusters, or does it prefer to grow in a solitary fashion? Is it so slimy that it keeps slipping out of your hands? And that's just for starters.

Let's say you're gazing at a mushroom's pink gills, and you think: Aha, pink spores. You could be completely wrong, since a mushroom's gills or pores sometimes have a different color from their spores. As spore color is useful in identifying a mushroom, you should learn how to make a spore print. To do so, remove a mushroom's cap from its stem and place it with the gill or pore surface face down on a

HOW TO MAKE A SPORE PRINT

1. *Remove the stalk and place the mushroom gill-side down on a piece of paper.*

Note: you can tape together white and black paper if you don't know if the spores will be light or dark.

2. *Cover the cap with a glass cup or bowl.*

3. *Leave the cap in position 2-6 hours or even overnight (ideal).*

3. *Voila! A spore print.*

piece of white paper. Then put a glass or bowl over it so that it won't dry out before it gets the chance to release its spores. Leave it overnight, and the next morning you'll probably see the outline of the mushroom's gills or pores in white, cream, red, rust-brown, salmon-pink, chocolate-brown or black on the paper. Not only will this give you a leg up on identifying your specimen, but you will have also created a quite engaging work of art...

Here I should add that, while *Fascinating Fungi of New England* will provide you with an introduction to selected New England species, you should also consult other mushroom guides. At the end of this book, there's a list of some particularly useful ones.

Mushrooming in New England

Despite its relatively small size, New England boasts a wide variety of habitats: from pine barrens to northern needleleaf forests, from beech-maple forests to pine-oak forests, from bogs to alpine communities, from coastal lowlands to glacial outwash plains and from windswept heaths to overgrown or not so overgrown pastures. Each of these habitats has its own range of mushroom species.

But let's not forget the urban areas, with their parks, mulched gardens, lawns and even waste areas. Certainly, mushrooms don't forget them. Each year I find 50 to 100 different species within a mile or so of my home in Cambridge, Massachusetts. Needless to say, there's not a forest in sight.

New England's mushroom season usually starts in the spring, although you can find a few species (polypores, jellies, crusts, etc.) year-round. During the spring, the best place to look for mushrooms is a hardwood forest. If it's late summer or fall, you should go to a coniferous or mixed forest. The season usually ends in November, but with global warming, all bets seem to be off. Recently, in January, I found some fresh *Russulas* and a few *Amanitas*, a fact that made me feel both pleased and sad.

Factors like wind, temperature, precipitation or lack thereof and a sudden hard frost can play havoc with normal fruiting patterns in New England as much as elsewhere. Sometimes, too, a mycelium can be exhausted from the previous year's exuberance, and it might be another few years before it has built up the energy to produce more mushrooms. Then there are the independent variables. I once found a polypore roughly ten times larger than normal on a stump near my house. The stump was being used by all the dogs in the neighborhood as a public lavatory, and the polypore's mycelium had turned the mega-amounts of nitrogen to its own advantage. Or such was my speculation.

Mushrooms often seem to delight in confusing us. Could they secretly be exchanging genes with each other? you might ask yourself, scratching your head. An antidote to head scratching is to join a mushroom club. In New England, there are several good ones (see the Resources section at the end of this book for more information). Such clubs offer forays, identification sessions, programs and much else. If there isn't a mushroom club in your area, then start one, and curious people like you will seem to appear out of nowhere... almost like mushrooms. Except, of course, none of these individuals will have been produced by a mycelium.

THE QUESTION OF EDIBILITY

Wild mushrooms are a delectable addition to a meal, but some mushrooms are poisonous, and they may resemble edible species. Eating them may make you sick or, in rare instances, be the death of you. It is your responsibility to identify any wild mushroom with 105 percent certainty before you eat it. If at all possible, your first few fungal forays should be with a knowledgeable and experienced mycologist.

Enthusiasm for mushroom hunting is often spurred by the hope of finding some wild delicacies for the table. Such enthusiasm must be moderated by care, experience and education. There's no need for a phobic fear of wild mushrooms, but it's important to be aware that certain mushrooms contain toxic compounds. Some of these toxins may be life threatening; others are less dangerous, but capable of giving an unwary eater's stomach a very unpleasant ride. Only those mushrooms that can be positively identified as good edibles should be eaten. A person may be guided by cultural familiarity with certain mushrooms. Formal classroom and field study with a knowledgeable teacher and use of detailed guidebooks can provide a basis for making accurate identifications. Some mushrooms are so distinctive that they make a good starting point for beginners eager to try wild mushrooms as food. Mushrooms, like other foods, can provoke individual allergic reactions, so an apt motto is "proceed with caution." Start with tiny portions to see how YOUR body reacts. The choice to eat wild mushrooms is an individual one. The individual who makes that choice is responsible for the consequences. This book is not intended to be a guide to edibility. Eat at your own risk!

HOW TO USE THIS BOOK

This book was written to introduce the curious amateur to the fascinating world of fungi. New England species come in a wide variety of sizes and shapes. In these pages, you'll encounter a species as beautiful as it is deadly, another shaped like an upside-down wasp's nest, and another that looks like a blackened tongue sticking out of the ground.

If I had included the thousands of fungi in New England, this book would not be useful as a field guide, although you could probably use it for bench pressing. But I have tried to include a generous sampling of common species, not-so-common species, downright weird species, highly colorful species and popular edibles. For the most part, I've skipped LBJs (Little Brown Jobs) as well as species that can only be distinguished microscopically. I've also skipped Athlete's Foot Fungus and ringworm. Sorry.

Fascinating Fungi of the New England is not organized by color or phylogenetic classification, but by six simple categories listed on the upper left hand page of each spread:

➤ **Gilled on Ground**
➤ **Gilled on Wood** (living trees, rotten logs, wood chips)
➤ **Gilled on Other** (pinecones, leaves, animal dung)
➤ **Non-gilled on Ground**
➤ **Non-gilled on Wood**
➤ **Non-gilled on Other**

When you find a species, try to place it in one of these categories. You may have to scrape away some soil to determine if it's growing on rotten wood just below the duff layer or actually growing on the ground. Note that what might seem like the ground to you might be extremely rotten wood to the fungus. Write down any distinctive features, then reach for your copy of *Fascinating Fungi of New England*. Happy hunting!

Each species is identified with the best known common name and the most recent scientific name.

This icon shows the color of a typical spore print. Shape, of course, will vary.

Check here for the category of mushroom (e.g. Gilled on Ground).

Sidebars provide interesting, unusual or simply amusing information about fungi.

Stylized icons show gill attachment. [See introduction for explanation of terms].

Captions point out identification traits to look for in the field.

Size icons show the range of cap widths and stalk heights.

Phenograms let you know when that fungus may be found in the field.

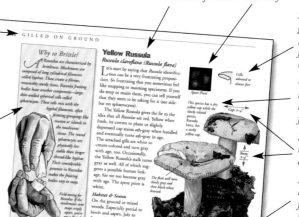

GILLED *on* GROUND

If someone says the word mushroom to you, you're likely to have a mental image of a gilled mushroom. It's the mushroom we drew in 2nd grade and the mushroom that invariably appears in cartoons. Put simply, it's got a cap with gills (lamellae) under it. Most, but not all gilled mushrooms have a stalk. All of them possess microscopic club-shaped basidia on their gills. Not a single one of them has any asci on its gills. But don't be disappointed: there are plenty of fungi with asci (ascomycetes) in other parts of this book.

You should note that gilled fungi delight in exchanging one color for another when they're drying out or aging. I've tried to indicate color changes whenever possible, but there's no law that requires a particular species to exhibit the color I've assigned to it. In all probability, it will exhibit that color, but there are exceptions to every fungal rule.

Check the base of any species you find to make sure that it's growing on the ground and not on buried wood. If it is growing on wood, see the next section— "Gilled Fungi on Wood."

Fly Agaric (Fly Amanita) *Amanita muscaria* var. *guessowii*

The iconic red-capped variety of *Amanita muscaria* tends to fruit in the West Coast, Siberia, and Europe, not to mention in comic books and animated films. In the eastern U.S., the only common variety of this well-distributed species is *Amanita muscaria* var. *guessowii*, which has a yellow to yellow-orange cap with occasional reddish tinges and a striate margin. Like other varieties, it has white to tannish warts on its cap. It also has close gills that can either be adnate or free, a skirtlike white ring on the stalk, and recurved scales toward the bottom of the stalk. At the very bottom of the stalk is a typical

White "warts" are actually remnant patches of the veil that once covered the developing mushroom.

Cap: 3–10"

Stem: 3–7"

Look for the ring on the stem.

July–Nov.

Gills: crowded and free

A yellow-orange cap is the signature of the variety 'guessowii' found on the East Coast. Caps may be as large as a dinner plate.

Fly Amanita

Spore Print

Amanita feature—a large more or less globose bulb. The spores are white.

Fungal Flyswatter

The name *Amanita muscaria* is derived from the belief that a saucer of milk with a few specimens resting in it will kill or at least stun flies. In Norway, the species is called *Rød Fluesopp* (Red Fly Mushroom), and in Germany, it's called *Fliegenpilz* (Fly Mushroom). The Russian name, *Mukhomor*, means Fly Killer, but it can also mean an old, decrepit person.

Santa's Vice

Saami (Lapp) shamans traditionally entered a trancelike state by eating the red-capped variety of *A. muscaria*. Reputedly, a shaman who'd eaten the mushroom acquired its distinctive red-and-white color scheme. Such shamans would visit their clients via the chimney, since snow usually made a front door entry impossible. Add to this the fact that reindeer take a well-documented delight in eating this mushroom, and that it makes you (and presumably reindeer) feel like they're flying, and a certain legendary fat guy will come to mind.

Leave the tripping to Santa, though. For the New England variety of this mushroom has the same alkaloids—ibotenic acid and muscimol—as the red-capped variety, but it usually has a much higher percentage of the former, which is toxic. So if you emulate Santa, it's likely that you'll give your stomach a good workout.

Habitat & Season

Single or in groups on the ground with hardwoods, especially oak and aspen. Common in urban and suburban areas. July to November.

Destroying Angel
Amanita bisporigera
(Amanita virosa)

Let's say you're wandering through the woods, and you suddenly see a ghostly white apparition rising up from the ground. In all probability, you're not seeing a Visitor From Beyond,

Look for a tattered, thin skirt-like ring on the upper stem.

Cap: 2–5"

Stem: 3–8"

July–Nov.

Destroying Angel

You may have to dig for it, but look for the large white volva that encases the stem base. It is often free at the upper edges and may be scalloped.

A sickly smell characterizes this species...and alerts you to your potential fate if you happen to eat it.

Lovely but Lethal

A full 90 percent of all fatal mushroom poisonings have been attributed to Amanitas and their amatoxins. Amatoxins cause severe, life threatening illness. If any portion of a mushroom that contains amatoxins is eaten, those powerful toxins block the vital production of new cells. Liver and kidney failure are not uncommon. The symptoms of the poisoning occur six to eight hours after the poisonous mushroom was eaten. First nausea, vomiting, fever and tremors manifest themselves. These may be bad enough to cause hospitalization, but they're temporary and may be passed off as a case of simple food poisoning. (That's why recent consumption of mushrooms should always be mentioned to the attending doctor) Three to six days later, however, there are signs of liver failure. Then these signs become a reality, followed by heart and brain failure. If it's any consolation, you can touch a deadly Amanita all you want with no adverse consequences.

but a Destroying Angel, a stately mushroom with a smooth white conic to ovoid cap. As befits an "angel," there are no warts on the cap. The thick, usually powdered or scaly stalk has a skirtlike, membranous veil around it. Often this veil is tattered, and in age it falls off. The stalk ends in a large club-shaped base that's surrounded by the saclike remnant of the universal veil (volva). Note that, as with any *Amanita*, you need to collect the entire mushroom, including the base, in order to identify it. The odor is distinctly unpleasant, rather like a hospital sickroom, which is doubtless where you'll end up if you happen to eat a Destroying Angel. The spore print is white.

Unangelic Behavior

The Destroying Angel is one of the most toxic mushrooms in the world. Don't think gastroenterological distress. Think severe liver and kidney damage from amatoxins that, among their other traits, shut down the basic machinery of cells (see sidebar for more information about amatoxins). Often a person who's dined on this mushroom can be saved only if he or she has a

liver transplant. Let me conclude with the reputed last words of a person who sautéed up a few Destroying Angels: "But they tasted so good..." [See sidebar on this page].

Russian Roulette

Conventional wisdom suggests that if a mushroom has been nibbled upon by one of our fellow creatures, then it's okay for us humans to eat it. With certain *Amanitas*, this is an invitation to a game of Russian roulette.

For many of those fellow creatures —rabbits, for example, and probably slugs—happily dine on *Amanita bisporigera* and the no less toxic *Amanita phalloides*, since their digestive systems can detoxify them. Other animals have no such ability. To quote mycologist David Moore: *"...while you are admiring the toothmarks around the margin of the dainty morsel you've just found, what makes you think the animal itself is not lying dead down a burrow somewhere?"*

Spore Print

Gills: crowded and free

Habitat & Season
Solitary or in groups in mixed woods.
July to November.

The Meixner Test

A possible way to test a mushroom for amatoxins is called the Meixner Test. Draw a circle on newsprint paper. Press the liquid out of a piece of fresh mushroom into the circle and allow it to dry. When dry, put a drop of concentrated hydrochloric acid on the circle. If amatoxins are present, a blue color will probably develop within 20 minutes. The more amatoxins present, the quicker the blue reaction.

Tawny Grisette *Amanita fulva*

Another very handsome member of the *Amanita* genus. It has a broadly bell-shaped cap, long tapering stem and pale sheath-like volva. The cap is orange, orange-brown to red brown with a smooth, usually glossy surface and deeply lined margin. Mature caps are flat with a raised center. The white to cream-colored gills are broad, closely packed under the cap and free from the stem. The mushroom's firm stem is tapered upward. It has a white, even surface with faint hints of cap color and a covering of very fine white hairs. The absence of a ring disproves the popular belief that all *Amanitas* have rings. A large, showy volva encloses the stem base. It is white to tan in color and its tissue is soft, delicate and easily torn. Spore color is white.

Spore Print

Gills: crowded and free

Habitat & Season
On the ground in coniferous and deciduous woods. July through September.

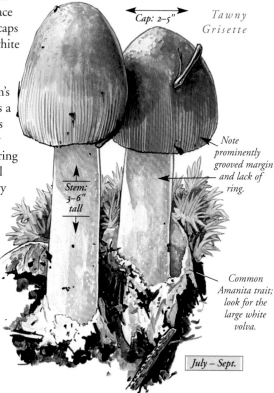

Cap: 2–5"

Tawny Grisette

Note prominently grooved margin and lack of ring.

Stem: 3–6" tall

Common Amanita trait; look for the large white volva.

July – Sept.

Citron Amanita
Amanita citrina

Probably the most common *Amanita* in New England, this species always seems to raise its spore-ridden cap when you're looking for other mushrooms. Perhaps it's trying to tell us that we should appreciate it even though it's not as obviously handsome as, for instance, its Fly Agaric cousin...

The light yellow to lemon-colored cap is convex to almost flat, with white cottony warts that often wash away in heavy rain. Gills are free, crowded, and white with occasional hints of cream or yellow. There's a flattened veil on the upper part of the stalk. As with most Amanitas, the stalk ends with a bulbous base.

Amanita citrina has one very distinctive feature—it smells like raw potatoes. Sometimes this smell is so strong that you wonder whether a specimen mightn't be a potato disguised as a mushroom. The spore print is white.

The bulbous base resembles a marshmallow.

Citron Amanita

Habitat & Season
On the ground in mixed woods. June to October or early November.

The gills usually smell like raw potatoes.

Cap: 2–4"

Stem: 3–6"

June – Oct.

The Blusher
Amanita rubescens

You might wonder why this species is called The Blusher. Does the fact that it's not poisonous make it feel like a wimp next to its toxic *Amanita* cousins? Or is it embarrassed because it's so susceptible to the designs of the *Amanita* mold (see below)? Neither of the above. The "blush" is a staining reaction that occurs when its flesh is bruised or in age. Note that this reaction sometimes occurs very slowly, so don't expect an immediate blush. Other features include: a convex whitish cap that's covered with gray, pinkish, or red warts; crowded, almost free white gills that develop reddish stains in age; a fragile, skirtlike whitish ring that appears torn in age; and a stalk that enlarges

Gills: crowded and free

Spore Print

downward to a usually elongated, reddish-staining basal bulb. The spores are (not red!) white.

The Blancher?
A variety of The Blusher with a light-colored cap and typically

whitish warts sometimes shows up in southern New England. It's known as *Amanita rubescens* var. *alba.*

Habitat & Season
Single or in groups on the ground in mixed woods. Commonly found with oak. June or July to October.

Cap: 2–6"

The Blusher

Stem: 3–8"

An easily embarrassed mushroom — The Blusher turns red if it's touched or bruised.

June – Oct.

A Moldy Outlook

*T*he *Amanita* mold (Hypomyces hyalinus) *turns* A. rubescens *into a phallic, chalky, pimpled mutation of its former self. The jury is out as to whether other Amanitas might be victimized by this parasite because the host is so completely altered by the parasite's sleight-of-hand. With* A. rubescens, *reddish stains identify the host.*

Why so Brittle?

All Russulas are characterized by brittleness. Mushrooms are composed of long cylindrical filaments called hyphae. These create a fibrous, reasonably sturdy tissue. Russula fruiting bodies have another component—large, thin-walled spherical cells called sphaerocysts. These cells mix with the hyphal filaments, often forming groupings like rosettes or islands in the mushroom tissue. The round sphaerocysts are physically less stable than longer thread-like hyphae. Their considerable presence in Russulas makes the fruiting bodies easy to snap.

Field-testing for Russulas: If the mushroom's stem snaps crisply apart, you've got a Russula

Yellow Russula
Russula claroflava (Russula flava)

Let's start by saying that *Russula* identification can be a very frustrating proposition. So frustrating that you sometimes feel like snapping or maiming specimens. If you do snap or maim them, you can tell yourself that they seem to be asking for it (see sidebar on sphaerocysts).

The Yellow Russula gives the lie to the idea that all *Russulas* are red. Yellow when fresh, its convex to plane or slightly depressed cap stains ash-gray when handled and eventually turns ash-gray in age. The attached gills are white to cream-colored and turn gray with age, too. Occasionally, the Yellow Russula's stalk turns gray as well. All of which suggests a possible human linkage, for we too become gray with age. The spore print is white.

Habitat & Season
On the ground in mixed woods. Especially partial to birch and aspen. July to September.

Spore Print

Gills: adnexed to almost free

This species has a dry yellow cap while the closely related species, Russula lutea, has a sticky yellow cap.

Cap: 2–4"

Stem: 2–4"

The flesh will turn slowly gray and then black when bruised.

Yellow Swamp Russula

Yellow Russula

July – Sept.

Emetic Russula
Russula emetica

Emetic Russula is probably a species complex—a group of species that share almost exactly the same features. Those features include: a bright red to reddish-orange cap that fades in age; close yellow-white gills; and a whitish stalk. As with most Russulas, you can peel the cuticle easily from the cap. The spore print is creamy or yellowish-white.

The Taste Test
The Emetic Russula has a characteristic that's implied by its species name—*emetic* means "that which induces vomiting." But even before an emetic reac-tion occurs, you'd by warned that something was amiss by *R. emetica's* incredibly acrid taste. Note: As long as you don't swallow it, you can taste a small piece of a *Russula* or its sister genus *Lactarius*, and if there's an acrid or peppery taste, you'll be in a better position to identify the specimen. Be sure you have one of these two genera before inaugurating a taste test!

Habitat & Season
Boggy areas in coniferous or mixed woods. Occasionally on very rotten wood. July or August to early October.

Cap may be convex, flat or slightly depressed.

"Slippery when wet" cap dries to shiny red.

Cap: 2–4"

Flesh crumbles easily, like chalk.

Emetic Russula

Stem: 2–3"

July – Oct.

Spore Print

Gills: adnexed to almost free

*Note that there are numerous red-capped, white-stemmed Russulas in the woods.

Field and Lab

Look-alike Russulas *can make field identification very difficult, but with lab work, you can often (but not always!) identify the species. Yet even if you can't identify the species, you'll discover an important microscopic feature—* Russula *spores are ornamented with little zigzag projections. Put a drop of the iodine solution called Melzer's reagent on these spores, and they'll turn a bluish color. This so-called amyloid reaction is another important feature of* Russulas. *In the field, a sure-fire way of determining if there are any* Russulas *in the vicinity is to look around for Indian Pipes* (Monotropa uniflo-ra). *This all-white plant, known as a myco-heterotroph, can't photosynthesize, so it engages in an illegal hook-up; it fastens its roots onto the mycelium of a* Russula *and absorbs nutrients that its host had intended to use for a very different purpose.*

Indian Pipe

Milky Mystery

How is it that a mushroom exudes "milk?" A number of mushrooms, particularly those commonly known as Milk Caps (Lactarius), *have specialized hyphae called lactifers. These large tubular structures store the thick fluid that oozes out when the flesh of those mushrooms is cut or injured. In* Lactarius *species, the tubu-*

lar milk-storing hyphae are long and have numerous branches that end in the tissues near the outer surface. When you cut them, they readily produce the "bleeding" effect. The fluid (latex) can be colorless or variously colored: blue, red, orange, yellow or white.

Orange Latex Milk Cap
Lactarius deterrimus (Lactarius deliciosus)

Depicted on a frieze from the ancient Roman city of Herculaneum as well as in a mural I once saw in Narssaq, Greenland, the Orange Latex Milky is a widely distributed species that grows almost exclusively with conifers. All parts are pinkish-orange to carrot-orange, but stain greenish when handled or in age. This includes the orange latex, too. The cap is robust, concentrically zoned, and convex, but eventually becomes vase-shaped or uplifted. Young speci-

mens have an inrolled margin. The crowded gills are attached to the stalk, which is usually pitted, white at the base and hollow in age. The last of these features makes this species a popular insect condominium. The spore print is cream to whitish-cream.

Habitat & Season
Solitary, scattered, or abundant under conifers, especially pine. July to late October.

Like many Lactarius *species, it becomes more vase-shaped the older it gets.*

Spore Print

Flesh stains green when bruised. Exudes orange latex when cut.

Note whitish bloom on young caps.

Orange Latex Milk Cap

Cap: 2–4"

Stem: 2–3"

| July | Aug. | Sept. | Oct. |

Indigo Milk Cap *Lactarius indigo*

I once saw perhaps a hundred Indigo Milkies next to a road outside Montpelier, Vermont, and in my excitement I nearly drove off the road. For Kingdom Fungi can boast very few blue mushrooms and even fewer as large and fleshy as this species. It's perhaps some consolation to less colorful species that the Indigo Milky fades to pale blue-gray in age.

Caps are depressed and concentrically zoned, with an inrolled margin when young. The bright blue gills are crowded and either attached or slightly decurrent. Stalks are firm, often tapered and hollow in age. The deep blue latex slowly turns greenish when it's exposed to air. The spore print is yellow or yellow-cream.

Cap: 2–6"

Stem: 1–3½"

Indigo Milk Cap

July–Oct.

Spore Print

Indigo-blue latex is exuded when any part is cut. Note decurrent gills.

Habitat & Season
Few to many on the ground in mixed woods. Often found with oak. July to October.

Peppery Milk Cap
Lactarius piperatus var. piperatus

This species tastes so hot that it puts the hottest curry to shame. Perhaps that taste is biochemical waste from its mycelium, or it makes insects less inclined to eat it. The robust cap is convex at first, then becomes depressed and funnel-shaped in age, while the inrolled margin becomes uplifted. The white adnate to slightly decurrent gills are so densely crowded that they look like a smooth surface... unless you're peering at them with a hand lens and see that they're repeatedly forked. Spore print is white.

Cap: 2–6"

Stem: 1–3"

July–Oct.

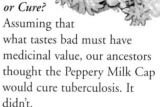

Spore Print

Poison or Cure?
Assuming that what tastes bad must have medicinal value, our ancestors thought the Peppery Milk Cap would cure tuberculosis. It didn't.

Habitat & Season Scattered or in small groups on the ground with hardwoods. July to October.

Matsutake
Tricholoma magnivelare (Armillaria ponderosa)

That New England has Matsutakes often surprises denizens of the West Coast, who seem to think this delectable mushroom is theirs and theirs alone. Truth to tell, Matsutakes weren't documented on the East Coast until fifty or so years ago, which may suggest that the species migrated from the West Coast. Or it may have simply been overlooked. From a distance, a Matsutake looks not unlike a number of large *Lactarius* or *Russula* species.

Robust would be a good word to describe this mushroom, at least on those occasions when you can see it. For Matsutakes often lie hidden in so-called mushrumps (forest duff pushed up by a fruiting body). Caps are convex to flat, with reddish-brown fibrils splayed against a white, then yellowish-brown background. The margin is inrolled at first, then uplifted in age. Covered by a membranous veil in the button stage, the gills are whitish (but staining light red or brown), attached or notched and usually crowded. The stalk is very solid with a persistent veil and narrowed base — its color tends to be white above the veil and pinkish below it. The odor has been described by mycologist David Arora as "a provocative compromise between 'red hots' and dirty socks." The spore print is white.

Mushroom Wars
In Japan, Matsutakes sell for prices that inspire North American mushroom pickers to lay claim to what they consider their own "patches." There's no commercial harvest in New England, so there haven't been any disputes over who owns which patch. Not so elsewhere. At a pickers' camp in British Columbia, I once observed a fight between two men. I assumed they were fighting over a Matsutake patch, but a third man set me straight. "Nah," he said. "They're fighting over a woman. I think they somehow got their priorities mixed up..."

Habitat & Season
Scattered on the ground with hemlock. Reported with pine. October and November.

Cap: 2–8"

Look for reddish or yellowish fibrils.

Stem: 2–6"

Fresh specimens have a spicy aroma.

Oct. – Nov.

Matsutakes are often buried under so-called mushrumps.

Matsutake

False Matsutake

Tricholoma caligatum (Armillaria caligata)

Often collected because of its resemblance to Matsutakes, but it's a wholly different species if not another (yet another!) species complex. In the field, it can be distinguished from its more celebrated cousin by its substrate (usually, but not always with hardwoods), its less fragrant odor, and the greenish mold *(Penicillium simplicissimum)* sometimes found at the base of its stalk. The hemispheric to plane cap has reddish-brown to gray-brown flattened scales against a white or pinkish background. The gills are white, attached, close and broad. The robust stalk tends to be large in the middle, tapering abruptly downward. The cinnamon-brown membranous veil initially flares upward, then collapses in age. Spore print is white.

Habitat & Season

Single or scattered on the ground with hardwoods. Less commonly with conifers. July to late October or early November.

False Matsutake

Note the abruptly tapering stem.

Cap: 2–5"

Stem: 2–4"

July – Oct.

Scientific vs. Common

Think of a mushroom as you might think of a person. Once you've learned a person's name, he or she will no longer be a stranger to you. And once you've learned a mushroom's name, it won't be a stranger, either. Unlike people, every mushroom has a common and a scientific name. Some of the common names are highly descriptive, like Shaggy Mane, Old Man of the Woods, Destroying Angel, and Stinky Squid. While mycologists prefer scientific names (Latin binomials), those names tend to be in a state of perpetual flux, and what's a (for instance) Coprinus one moment might be a Coprinopsis the next. That's because DNA analysis has determined that mushrooms that look alike aren't necessarily related to each other. In other words, two very different species could have developed some arcane feature like turning to an inky mess independently of each other.

In this book, I've used the most accepted common names in New England, and if a species doesn't have a common name, I've made up one that indicates one of its most distinctive features. For example, Byssocorticium atrovirens is blue-gray in color, so I've called it the Blue-gray Crust. For the scientific name, I've used the most widely accepted one at the time of this writing.

The Rooter *Xerula furfuracea*
(*Oudemansiella radicata*)

The Rooter's most diagnostic feature is a long rooting stalk that tapers to a point. This atypical stalk is sometimes attached to wood buried in the ground. Deep in the ground: I once collected a specimen with a 29-inch stalk, which caused my jaw as well as the jaws of my fellow foragers to drop in unison.

This species has a wrinkled brown or grayish cap with a round knob or umbo. Its white gills are distant and attached to the stalk, but often free in age. The stalk itself often has dark fibers as well as dark longitudinal lines. Note that it's slightly enlarged toward the base, too. Also note that it's somewhat brittle, so dig carefully if you want to marvel at its full length. The spores are white.

X. furfuracea is easily identified by its slender stature and very distinctive long tapering "root" that extends into the ground.

Habitat & Season
On the ground with hardwoods. Solitary, scattered or in groups near old stumps or decaying deciduous logs, especially beech. Probably saprobic as well as mycorrhizal. July to October.

The Rooter

Cap: 1–5"

Look for wrinkles radiating from the center.

Stem: 3–12"

Hard to miss: Note the unusually long, graceful stem that tapers toward the top.

July – Oct.

Gills: well separated and free

Spore Print

Wine-cap Stropharia
Stropharia rugosoannulata

The Wine Cap usually has a large bell-shaped maroon-red to chestnut-brown cap, although yellowish caps —Chardonnays?—have been known to occur. The gills are crowded, adnate, and at first whitish, but soon become grayish-black and then purple-black as the spores mature. Around the stem there's a membranous ring whose upper surface is grooved and whose lower surface seems to have small claws. The stalk is robust and whitish, with occasional brown stains. At the bottom of its bulbous base are massed white mycelial threads known as rhizomorphs. It's thought that the Wine Cap is an exotic species brought to the U.S. many years ago on imported bark mulch. The spores are purplish-black.

Habitat & Season
Scattered to numerous on wood chips, in mulch or straw, on lawns, and cultivated areas. It has a very long growing season—May to November.

Cap: 2–9"

Wine-cap Stropharia

Stem: 3–8"

May – Nov.

The stalk has a partial white veil that leaves a persistent membranous ring with claw-like points.

The Wine Cap's favorite habitat is wood chips or mulch.

Spore Print

Gills: adnate and closely spaced

Big Cat
Catathelasma ventricosa

This species is so robust and its flesh so firm that if it were a Major League Baseball player, it would doubtless be investigated for steroid use. Its cap is convex, off-white to grayish and smooth, but somewhat scaly in age. The gills are decurrent, close to nearly distant and white to off-white or buff. The stem has a prominent, two-layered flaring ring. That stem is also white to yellowish, swollen in the middle (ventricosa means "big-bellied") and tapers to a point below ground. Mycorrhizal with spruce, the Big Cat affixes itself to its host via an extremely large (3-inch to 10-inch) stemlike root. The spore print is white.

Habitat & Season
Single to several on the ground with spruce. Occasionally with balsam fir. August to late October.

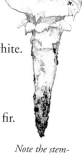

Note the stem-like root

Ventricosa *means "big-bellied" —the stem is typically swollen in the middle.*

Cap: 3–7"

Big Cat

Aug. – Oct.

Stem: 2–4"

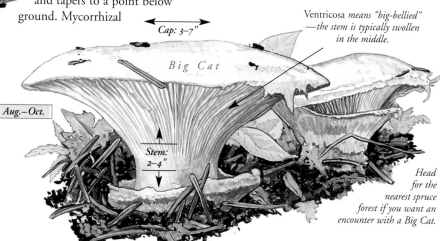

Head for the nearest spruce forest if you want an encounter with a Big Cat.

Lawnmower's Mushroom
Panaeolus foenisecii (Psathyrella foenisecii)

This common lawn inhabitant is probably the most popular edible mushroom with toddlers at the grazing stage. That it can be hallucinogenic may or may not be of interest to the toddler. I say "can be hallucinogenic" because some specimens have the tryptamine derivatives psilocybin and psilocin in small quantities, and some do not. The "high" conferred by these derivatives is so mild that only a toddler, or a dog, is likely to experience it.

The reddish-brown or dark brown cap is bell-shaped to conical when fresh, becoming plane and grayish-brown or tan in age. For this fragile and short-lived mushroom, age may mean the same day in which it fruited.

The gills are adnate to almost free, relatively close and pallid to light brown, but deep purple-brown or chocolate-brown at maturity. The brittle off-white stalk enlarges slightly downward and usually becomes brown from the base upward in age. The spores are dark brown to dark purple-brown.

Habitat & Season
Scattered to numerous in grassy areas like lawns, golf courses, parks, cemeteries, baseball fields, etc. May to October.

Lawnmower's Mushroom

Cap: ½–1½"

Stem
¼–?

May–Oct.

The Lawnmower's Mushroom is commonly found on (surprise!) lawns.

Magic Mushrooms

One of this book's themes is that all mushrooms, even poisonous ones, are magical. So potent is their magic that you can get turned on simply by foraging for them. Another of its themes is that you shouldn't pop a mushroom into your mouth too soon after you've first made its acquaintance. This is just as true for a species that might be called a "magic mushroom" (or 'shroom) as it is for an apparent edible. With respect to the former, ignorance might lead to bliss, but it also might lead to a pumped stomach... or worse. The not necessarily common *Psilocybe* species in New England have some very common look-alikes that are potentially deadly—need I say more? Well, I will say a bit more: the law may or may not be a reasonable one, but the Comprehensive Drug Abuse and Control Act prohibits the possession of psilocybin mushrooms and/or capsules. It's hard to go looking for mushrooms in jail.

Common Laccaria
Laccaria laccata

Called a weed by some mycologists because it has the ability to fruit almost anywhere, but weeds are seldom as variable in shape and color as the Common Laccaria. It can have a red, pink, orangish, or brown convex to centrally depressed cap, but you can multiply these colors logarithmically when the cap begins to fade. The gill attachment is usually but not always adnate, and the usually but not always distant gills have a pallid pink, pallid reddish, or flesh-colored variation on the cap color. The stalk is dry, fibrous and colored like the cap, whatever color that is. The stalk may or may not have a small bulb at the base. Not surprisingly, there may be as many as fifteen or twenty different species known as *Laccaria laccata*, according to Laccariologist Greg Mueller. The spore print is white.

Common Laccaria

Cap: ½–2½"

Stem: ½–4"

Pinkish gills are typical of Laccarias.

July–Nov.

Habitat & Season

Scattered or groups in swampy/mossy areas as well as waste places or places with poor sandy soil. Also in the woods with, primarily, hardwoods. June to November.

Look for this species especially in areas with poor soil.

Viscid Violet Cort
Cortinarius iodes

Cortinarius iodes is slimy in wet weather, so slimy that once you remove it from the ground, it'll cling to your fingers. Another distinctive feature is a convex purplish cap decorated with yellowish splotches. Note, however, that

Viscid Violet Cort

Cap: 1–3" wide

Cap and stem slimy when wet.

The stem is often bulbous at the base.

Stem: 1–3" tall

July – Sept.

both the cap and the purple gills fade in age, the former to a silver-lilac color and the latter to grayish-cinnamon. Faded or not, the gills are attached, close and broad. The stem has a cobwebby veil on its upper part and is usually enlarged downward. A similar species, the Purple Cort (*Cortinarius violaceus*), has a fibrillose cap, along with a darker purplish color that doesn't fade in age. The spores of both species are rusty-brown.

Habitat & Season

Scattered or in small groups under hardwoods, especially oak and beech. July to September or early October.

Gills: adnate and closely spaced   *Spore Print*

Typical Cort *Cortinarius* species

Although *Cortinarius* species can be difficult to identify, the genus itself has certain features that proclaim, "Hi, I'm a Cort." For example, young specimens typically have a cobwebby veil (cortina) connecting the cap to the stalk. The cap itself is usually convex to broadly convex and firm. Gills are adnate, closely spaced, and rust-colored or brownish when the spores are mature. The stalk tends to be relatively short and usually has a rimmed basal bulb at the bottom. All bets are off with

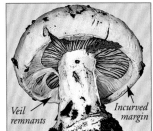

Note the incurved margin, cobwebby veil and how the close-set gills attach to the stem — common traits of young Corts.

Veil remnants   *Incurved margin*

respect to the color, though. Corts can be purplish, brown, orange, gray, blackish and red as well as all the colors in-between. The spores are rusty-brown or brown.

Habitat & Season

On the ground with hardwoods or conifers. June to October or early November.

Cap: 2–4"

Typical Cort

Stem: 1–3"

June – Oct.

Spore Print

Gills: adnate and closely spaced

Red-gilled Cort *Dermocybe semisanguineus (Cortinarius semisanguineus)*

To my mind, this Cort has one of the nicest umbos of any species—not too big, not too small, and usually so perfectly proportioned that you feel like touching it. It sits proudly on top of a bell-shaped to convex, yellowish-cinnamon, minutely hairy cap. But the species' gills are hardly less attractive than its umbo. They're broadly attached to the stalk, crowded, and a striking blood-red color. The stalk is pale at the top, reddish at the base, and yellowish inbetween, with a fibrillose zone where the cortina used to be. Not to be confused with the Blood Red Cort (*Dermocybe sanguineus*), which has a bright red cap. The spore print of both species is rusty brown.

Diagnostic feature —a pronounced umbo or nipple

Cap: 1–2½"

Stem: 1–3"

Note the distinctive reddish-colored gills.

June–Nov.

Red-gilled Cort

Dyeing Breed
The Red-gilled Cort is among the very best of all dye mushrooms. When cooked with alum as a mordant, it yields a rich yellow or red dye.

Habitat & Season
Scattered to numerous on the ground with hardwoods and conifers. Often growing on moss. June to November.

Spore Print

Gills: adnate and closely spaced

Capturing a Mushroom's Color

Beautiful colors can be extracted from fungi… but not necessarily the color of the mushroom. For instance, Jack O'Lanterns are orange, but they often yield a purplish dye. Here's how you can make mushroom dye: In a large pot (not aluminum), heat 2 to 3 quarts of water and 10 grams of alum. The wools or other fibers are put into the hot (not boiling) water and set aside for one hour. Meanwhile, the mushrooms (about a quart) are boiled in 2-3 quarts of water for one hour, then allowed to cool slightly. The wools/fibers are then carefully drained and placed in the hot mushroom liquid together with the mushrooms. Steep one hour, stirring occasionally. Wools/fibers are then carefully rinsed. Add one cup of vinegar to one rinse. Give the material a final rinse and hang to dry out of the direct sun. Then get out your knitting needles!

Witch's Hat
Hygrophorus conicus (Hygrocybe conica)

This mushroom's conical cap with its pointed central peak suggests a witch's hat—hence its common name. Unlike most actual witch's hats, however, the cap may be variously colored: bright red, red-orange or yellow with hints of green. It is thin, fragile and translucent with a smooth surface. When moist, it is somewhat sticky. The cap edge is striate and often splits as the fruiting body matures. The closely spaced yellow gills are thick, soft and waxy. They eventually become torn or frayed. The delicate cylindrical stem is colored like the cap and may be twisted or longitudinally lined. White mycelium lies at the stem base.

A diagnostic characteristic of this mushroom is that it blackens readily when bruised or with age. The spore print is white.

Cap: 1–3"

Habitat & Season
Single or in groups on the ground under conifers. July to September.

Stem: 1–4"

Note longitudinal lines on stem.

June – Sept.

Witch's Hat

The Witch's Hat will blacken when bruised. You may find all black specimens in the field.

Spore Print

Gills: free and well spaced

Scarlet Waxy Cap
Hygrocybe coccinea

*H*ygrocybes specialize in brightly-colored caps, and this species is no exception. Its cap is an intense scarlet with yellowish tints. At first bell-shaped, it soon becomes flat, albeit flat with a flaring margin and a modest umbo. The waxy gills are yellowish or orange-red, attached and usually crowded. The stalk is smooth, hollow, yellow-orange to orange-red and somewhat paler toward the bottom. The flesh is very fragile. The gills of the Fading Scarlet Waxy Cap (*Hygrocybe miniata*) become a pallid yellow in age. All *Hygrocybe* species have a white spore print.

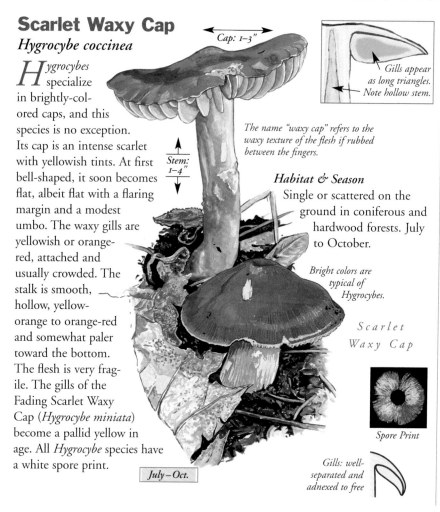

Cap: 1–3"

Stem: 1–4"

Gills appear as long triangles. Note hollow stem.

The name "waxy cap" refers to the waxy texture of the flesh if rubbed between the fingers.

Habitat & Season
Single or scattered on the ground in coniferous and hardwood forests. July to October.

Bright colors are typical of Hygrocybes.

Scarlet Waxy Cap

Spore Print

July – Oct.

Gills: well-separated and adnexed to free

Dunce Cap
Conocybe lactea

*A*nother common lawn inhabitant with a short life expectancy. Troops of Dunce Caps fruit overnight on dew-laden grass, and by the middle of the next day, they've shriveled up. Yet this seemingly delicate mushroom has an indelicate side. An antifeedant toxin in its hyphae disposes of any nematodes looking for a hyphal meal. Unlike the oyster mushroom, it doesn't dine on its victims. Killing them is sufficient. Given such behavior, might The Terminator be a better common name than Dunce Cap?

The species' light tan conical cap is often tinged with yellow at the top and striate or slightly wrinkled when moist. The flesh is thin and brittle. Gills are whitish when young, but turn yellowish-brown to brown as the spores mature. The stalk is white, thin, and has no ring. By contrast, the potentially deadly *Conocybe filaris* has a large movable ring. All *Conocybes* have a light brown spore print.

Habitat & Season

In troops on lawns and other grassy areas. May to September.

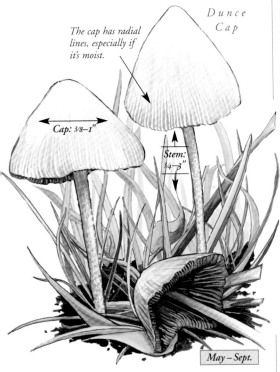

Dunce Cap

The cap has radial lines, especially if it's moist.

Cap: ⅜–1"

Stem: ¾–3"

May – Sept.

More delicate than duncelike—most Dunce Caps shrivel up by mid-day.

Blewit *Lepista nuda (Clitocybe nuda)*

Don't feel like you blew it if it's late October, and you haven't found any Blewits. For *Lepista nuda* seems to like cool or even cold weather. In early December, I once collected perhaps fifty Blewits near a half-frozen lake with snow flurries twirling through the air.

Caps are convex with an inrolled margin, smooth, glossy looking, and lilac-purple to purplish-gray, becoming brownish to tan. In age, they become uplifted and wavy, even jaunty, which probably explains their name (Blewit=blue hat). The broad, adnate gills fade with age from lilac, purple or grayish-purple to tan or brownish-tan. The solid stem is colored like the gills and slightly scurfy, ending in an enlarged base with purplish mycelial hairs. The odor when fresh resembles anise. In my humble opinion, their flavor resembles ambrosia.

Because Blewits look like Corts, you should get a spore print if you have any doubt about what you've collected. *Cortinarius* spores are brownish, while the spores of a Blewit are pinkish or pinkish-buff.

Habitat & Season

Single or in clustered groups in humus-rich ground, sawdust, or compost piles. Also in meadows or on the ground under both hardwoods and conifers. August to November, sometimes into December.

Gills: adnate, closely spaced and sometimes notched

Spore Print

Blewit

Blewit in its prime

Cap: 2–6"

Blewit past prime

Stem: 1–3"

Aug.–Nov.

Alcohol Inky (Tippler's Bane) *Coprinopsis atramentarius (Coprinus atramentarius)*

Tight clusters of these glossy, lead-gray mushrooms appear in gardens, on stumps and in grassy places enriched by buried woody debris. Young caps are egg-shaped with margins puckered and pressed against the stem. At maturity, the mushrooms are bell-shaped with a grooved, splitting margin. Cap flesh is thin and pallid. The gills are set very close together, broad and initially white in color but turning dark. The cylindrical, silky-white stem is hollow. A dark zone of veil material rings the lower stem. The spores are black but you usually get a blackish goo rather than a spore print.

Self-destructive Behavior

Inky Caps have a unique method of dispersing their spores. Their gills are so crowded that they can't free their spores, so they turn themselves into globs of ink. This self-digestion progresses from the margin to the stem, freeing the mature black spores. In the end, all that's left is a black gooey mess.

Booby Trap

Mycologist Bryce Kendrick calls *C. atramentarius* a "booby trap for drinkers."

Coprine is a unique amino acid manufactured by the Alcohol Inky. It is not itself a poison, but it causes considerable problems for anyone who consumes an alcoholic beverage within 48 hours of eating the mushroom. The unfortunate drinker will face the outset of alarming symptoms; flushing of face and neck, swelling and numbness of hands and face, rapid heartbeat, tingling extremities, nausea and vomiting. Coprine, which persists a long time in the diner's system after eating, blocks the body's metabolism of ethyl alcohol, stopping the process at the acetaldehyde stage. Acetaldehyde is the poison causing the symptoms. It

Coprinus species begin dissolving from the margin.

Note the dark zone of veil material

Alcohol Inky

Cap: 3/4–3½"

Stem: 1–4"

May – Nov.

One of the earliest gilled fungi of the season.

should be noted that the symptoms of coprine poisoning disappear on their own without treatment.

Habitat & Season

Clustered on woody debris in lawns, parks, gardens, residential areas and city dumps. Also at the base of unhealthy hardwood trees. May to November.

"Autodeliquescence:" these inky caps will soon be liquid. This liquid was once used as writing ink!

Gills: free and closely spaced

Spore Print

Shaggy Mane
Coprinus comatus

"Shags" often seem to pop up spontaneously after a rain. The cap of the young mushroom is tall, column-like to oval with a smooth, white to ochre surface and a margin pressing against the stem. The maturing mushroom expands to become bell-shaped, with a lined, often tattered, margin. The cap's white outer skin (cuticle) breaks into broad, overlapping scales whose edges tend to fray and curl upward, giving the mushroom a "shaggy dog" appearance. White gills are free, narrow and densely packed under the cap. There is often a delicate pinkish tint in the gills. The silky, white stem is cylindrical and hollow, with a thin, movable ring. The base of the stem is enlarged, pointed and rooting. Like other inky caps, Shaggy Manes disperse their spores by a gradual dissolving of cap and gill tissue. This is an easily recognized species with its column-like form and a copiously scaly cap that looks quite shabby in age. The spores are black.

Habitat & Season

Scattered or in dense clusters in urban areas, especially on wood chips, packed soil or compost heaps. Also along roadsides, trails and other disturbed areas. May to November.

Gills: free and closely spaced

Cap: 1¼ – 2½"

Shaggy Mane

Cap: up to 6"

Scaly cap surface helps distinguish this species from the Alcohol Inky.

Strong? They've been known to push up through asphalt.

Stem: 3–9"

June – Oct.

Spores black; but you usually get a black gooey mess rather than a spore print.

Japanese Umbrella Inky
Parasola plicatilis

There are no hard and fast fungal rules. Most Inky Caps deliquesce… most, but not all. Consider this species. It's so thin-fleshed that it tends to dry up rather than liquefy.

The delicate cap is pleated (grooved) nearly to the center. Narrow gills are grayish, becoming black, and attached to a collar at the top of the stem. The stem itself is whitish, hollow, and fragile. Indeed, the entire fruiting body is so fragile that if you collect it, you usually won't be able to get it home in one piece. The spore print is black.

Habitat and Season
Single to scattered on lawns and in grassy areas. May to October.

Spore Print

Cap: ½–2"

Stem: 1–3"

Japanese Umbrella

Shaggy Parasol
Macrolepiota rachodes

If this species was an actual parasol, the scales on its cap would tell you that it was in need of repair. For they're coarse, pinkish, and seemingly ready to fall off. Their arrangement in concentric circles on an underlying whitish cap surface is somewhat less askew. The gills are free, close, usually broad, and white, although they stain brown when bruised or in age. The stalk is smooth, bruises brownish, and has a membranous ring near the top. This ring is movable, so you can amuse yourself by raising or lowering it on the stalk. The Parasol *(Macrolepiota procera)* is similar, but has small brownish scales on its stalk and typically doesn't bruise. The spores of both species are white.

Habitat & Season
Single to numerous in wood chips, along the side of roads, or in cultivated areas

Cap: 2⅜–8"

Shaggy Parasol

Note moveable, thick white annulus.

Stem: 4–8"

Sept. – Nov.

and gardens. Often in fairy rings in grassy places. September to November.

Gills: free and closely spaced

Spore Print

Fairy Rings

When there's a relatively even distribution of nutrients in a habitat like a lawn or a cemetery, a mycelium will often grow outward at a relatively even rate. The circular pattern of mushrooms produced by this mycelium's outer fringes is known as a fairy ring in English-speaking countries or a witch's ring in Germany and Central Europe. Depending on conditions, a fairy ring can grow in circumference a few inches or a few feet every year. One particularly large fairy ring is at Stonehenge in southeastern England; it's estimated to be at least a thousand years old. The best-known fairy ring mushroom is Marasmius oreades, *but several others, including the Meadow Mushroom (*Agaricus campestris*), are also capable of this growth pattern.*

Meadow Mushroom
Agaricus campestris

When mature, it has grayish-black or blackish gills.

Stem: 1– 2½"

Cap: 1–5"

The wild sister of the common supermarket button mushroom.

Meadow Mushroom

Gills: free and closely spaced

Spore Print

June – Sept.

One of the most widely picked mushrooms in the world, the Meadow Mushroom is known as *zampion polni* (field mushroom) in Slovakia, *pai-chin* (white mushroom) in China and (no lascivious grins now) *pink bottoms* in England. It appears in arcs, fairy rings or scattered groups primarily in grassy areas. The smooth whitish cap is typically dome-shaped, becoming flatter with age. The cap's center (disk) is often darkened by soft, gray-brown hairs or scales, which are especially evident during dry periods. It does not stain when bruised. Look for frayed veil remnants; they're often found hanging from the strongly down-turned cap. Delicately pink when young, the gills are free, narrow and crowded. As the mushroom expands, the gills become bright pink and eventually, with spore production, chocolate-brown. The solid stem is short, giving the mushroom a squat appearance. The stem is dry and smooth above a narrow ring that often wears away. The stem surface below the ring is covered with fine fibers. Spore print is brownish black.

Supermarket Fare

The white, fleshy button mushroom commonly found in supermarkets is *Agaricus bisporus*—a commercially grown relative of the Meadow Mushroom. The primary difference is microscopic. In the case of *A. bisporus*, there are two spores per basidium; *A. campestris* usually has four spores. By such seemingly minute differences do different species proclaim themselves.

Habitat & Season

Single, scattered or abundant in lawns, baseball fields, pastures, cemeteries, golf courses and (of course) meadows. June to September.

GILLED
on WOOD

As often as not, gilled mushrooms that grow on wood seem to grow in large clusters joined at the base (mycological term: caespitose), or close together over a small area (mycological term: gregarious), or scattered over a large area. The smaller the species, the more likely you'll see dozens of them... or in the case of the so-called Fuzzy Foot, hundreds of them. Large species like the Broad Gill seem happy to be by themselves.

Most gilled mushrooms that grow on wood are saprobic, dining off dead tissue on living trees or dead tissue on logs, snags or stumps. The major exception to this eating habit is the Honey Mushroom, which can be a virulent parasite on living trees. Honeys can also be virulent saprobes on dead and dying trees.

Some gilled mushrooms seem to be growing on the ground rather than wood, but mushrooms like to fool us, and often the wood is buried. The Jack O'Lantern and the Broad Gill practice this sort of foolery. Then there are the impartial species such as the Twisted Entoloma: they can grow on the ground, but they can also grow on rotten wood.

Bleeding Mycena
Mycena haematopus

If you break, squeeze, or otherwise injure this common species, you'll end up with drops of blood-red latex on your fingers. Whereupon you can turn to your companions and say with a pronounced English accent, "Look, it's another Bleedin' Mycena..."

The caps of this delicate species are reddish, pinkish-brown, or purplish-gray and bell-shaped to conic with a dark umbo, but usually becoming convex in age. Gills are attached, crowded, and stain red if injured (a burrowing springtail counts as an injury). The hollow stalk is hairy at first, but—like so many of us—it loses its hair with age. Even so, some coarse white hairs remain at the very bottom of the stalk. The spore print is white.

Habitat & Season
Solitary or in clusters on hardwood stumps and logs. June to November, but also in the winter during mild spells.

Cap: 1–2"

Stem: 1–4"

June–Nov.

Look for Bleeding Mycena singly or—more commonly—clustered on decaying wood

Gills: varied and adnate

Spore Print

Fungus-eat-fungus

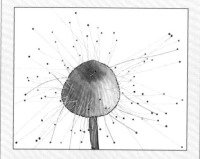

*I*n the volatile fungal world, you will frequently come across mushrooms enveloped in a cottony coat of mold, or "painted" white or some lurid color by the presence of another fungus. Such parasites can be very specific as to the host mushroom. That host is at once a habitat and a food source; without it, the parasite could not survive.

Here Spinellus fusiger, *a fungus related to bread molds, has given a Bleeding Mycena a punk haircut. The dark balls at the end of the hair-like stalks contain its spores. Spinellus fusiger allows the host to disperse its spores—guaranteeing itself future hosts—but eventually reduces the* Mycena *to a puddly soup.*

Pinwheel Marasmius
Marasmius rotula

Clusters of these delicate musrooms commonly grow on decaying deciduous wood. Each cap is parasol-shaped with a broad central depression. The cap surface is dry, parchment-like, with an arrangement of pleats extending almost to the scalloped margin. Distant white gills are attached to a collar (collarium) that is itself attached to the black stem. Another *Marasmius* species, *M. scorodonius*, smells strongly of garlic.

Resurrection!
Shriveled and inconspicuous, *Marasmius* species are rarely noticed during dry weather, but after rainy periods the tiny fungi revive—hence the nickname "resurrection fungi."

Habitat & Season
In dense clusters on decaying wood, especially beech. May to October.

Cap: 5/8 – 3/4"

Look for a translucent area at the top of the stem.

Stem: 5/8 – 3"

Pinwheel Marasmius

May – Oct.

Gills: Adnate and attached at collar

Fuzzy Foot
Xeromphalina campanella

There's probably no such thing as a Fuzzy Foot. Instead, there are Fuzzy Feet, hundreds of them covering a coniferous log from end to end. Such teeming multitudes would provide a mushroom podiatrist with a very comfortable living.

The convex cap is reddish-brown or orange-brown, but becomes a pallid yellow in age. It has a central depression that sometimes serves as a tiny swimming pool for even tinier insects. The decurrent yellowish gills have cross-veins (see inset). The stalk is yellowish toward the top, reddish-brown toward the base and usually curved. At its base are bright tawny hairs. Of course, they're strands of hyphae, not hairs, but "Strands of Hyphae Foot" is neither a memorable nor a very euphonious common name. Spores are light buff.

Look for cross-veins: small, intersecting ridges between the gills.

Habitat & Season
In huge clusters on decaying coniferous logs. May to November.

Cap: ⅛ – 1⅜"

Fuzzy Foot is so specialized in its choice of host that a fruiting confirms that the stump or log is a conifer.

Stem: ⅝–3"

Gills: decurrent and spaced

These fungi have fuzzy feet! Look for the dense tuft of hairs at the base of the stalk.

Fuzzy Foot

May – Nov.

Jack O'Lantern
Omphalotus olearius

Jack O'Lanterns are robust bright orange mushrooms that grow in tight clusters on stumps, on the roots of living trees and on buried wood. Mature caps are convex, but become increasingly flattened and sometimes depressed with age. Often they'll display a small umbo. The cap's surface is smooth, but streaked with small fibrils. The margin is incurved, wavy and occasionally splits with age. The gills are close, yellow-orange and extend down the stalk. The stalk is centrally to laterally attached, colored like the cap, smooth and tapering. Older specimens have downy or scaly stalks. The spores are whitish-cream.

Don't be a Jackass
Jack O'Lanterns are a common cause of mushroom poisoning in New England because of their apparent similarity to chanterelles. But chanterelles have ridges, not gills. If you mistake gills for ridges, expect some combination of the following: nausea, vomiting, abdominal pain, diarrhea and sweating. You won't

need hospitalization, but you will need to look more closely at mushrooms.

Habitat & Season

In clusters at the base of hardwood trees and stumps. Especially common with oak. July or August to November.

Gills: decurrent and crowded

Spore Print

Jack O'Lantern

Cap: 2–8"

Stem: 2–8"

Called Jack O'Lantern because it may glow in the dark. But, the emitted light is greenish, not orange.

Inexperienced mushroomers may mistake this species for chanterelles. But note the sharp-edged gills, dense clustered growth on wood; characteristics not shared with the chanterelles.

July–Nov.

An Eerie Green Light in the Night

Like several other mushrooms, the aptly named Jack O'Lantern emits a greenish glow in the dark. You can see this glow on a moonless night or, if you carry a specimen home, in a totally darkened room, The glow lasts 40 to 50 hours after the specimen is collected and is usually bright enough for you to see each individual gill.

In Huckleberry Finn, Huck and Tom succeed in digging a tunnel by using a bioluminescent fungus as their source of light. Mark Twain calls this fungus "foxfire." There are also stories of people reading by the light of a glowing fungus or its glowing mycelium. I've tried this with at least half a dozen different bioluminescent species, but I haven't succeeded in reading yet.

How does a mushroom manage to produce light? The short answer: it produces a pigment called luciferin that, upon being oxidized by the enzyme luciferase, emits light. It's still a mystery as to why fungi glow in the dark, but maybe they're trying to get night-flying insects to spread their spores. Or maybe the glow is simply a byproduct of wood degradation. Or maybe the light activates DNA repair, as it does with bioluminescent bacteria.

Deadly Galerina
Galerina autumnalis

*G*alerina autumnalis gives the lie to the popular belief that any fungal species that grows on wood is edible, for it contains deadly phallotoxins as well as amatoxins (see sidebar on pg. 18). That something as small as a single *Galerina autumnalis* can kill something as large as a human being indicates that size really doesn't matter in Nature.

The convex to plane cap is brown, reddish-brown or dark brown when young, but tan or yellowish-tan in age. In wet weather, it's somewhat viscid, and the margin is striate. The gills are crowded, broad and at first yellowish-brown, becoming rusty-brown or brown. The stalk is dry, hollow and light brown to brown, with a membranous ring or at least a membranous zone if the ring itself has disappeared. This is a species where a spore print might make a big difference in your life. The spore color of *G. autumnalis* is rusty-brown.

Habitat & Season
Scattered to numerous on stumps and logs. Prefers hardwoods, but also found on coniferous wood. September to November, but occasionally fruits in May and June, too.

Deadly Galerina

The cap is radially lined when moist.

Cap: ½ – 2½"

Note a ring or membraneous zone.

Stem: 1–4"

Sept. – Nov.
Sometimes May and June

Always grows individually, never in crowded bunches like (for example) the Honey Mushroom.

Big Laughing Gym
Gymnopilus spectabilis

*T*his species is called the Big Laughing Mushroom not because it laughs at your attempts to identify it, but because its psilocybin and/or psilocin content induces, among other reactions, uncontrollable laughter. There's a well-known incident of a woman who'd eaten the mushroom by mistake. As she was being driven to the hospital, she laughed heartily and said, "if this is how you die from mushroom poisoning, I'm all for it." Reactions can be variable, however. One man who'd eaten a meal of Big Laughing Mushrooms suffered from priapism (think severe overdose of Viagra®) for three days—no laughing matter!

Gymnopilus spectabilis caps are orange-yellow to bright orange and convex when young, but nearly plane in age. They're also smooth when

Gills: adnate and closely spaced

Spore Print

Big Laughing Gym

Cap: 3–7"

Aug.–Oct.

Sneaky behavior —often it would like you to think that it's growing on the ground, but it's really growing on buried wood.

Twisted Entoloma
Entoloma strictius (strictior)

Twisted Entoloma is one of the earliest fleshy fungal fructifications to appear in the spring. The cap is convex to conical, occasionally with a pointed umbo. Cap

Cap: 1–4"

Stem: 2–4"

The twisted longitudinal lines on the stem give this species its common name.

April–Aug.

Twisted Entoloma

A spring mushroom—the umbo helps it push up last year's leaf and needle litter when it's first emerging from the ground.

young, but scaly or fibrous in age. The gills are crowded, adnate to slightly decurrent and yellowish or orangish, but turn rust-colored as the spores mature. The stem is colored like the cap and more or less club-shaped, with a ring that collapses or falls off in age. The taste is extremely bitter. You might confuse this species with a Jack O'Lantern, but its spores are white or yellow-tinted, while a Laughing Mushroom's spores are rusty-brown.

Habitat & Season
Single or in clusters on dead or decaying hardwoods. Sometimes on buried wood. August to October.

color is gray-brown, dark brown, tan, and occasionally reddish, drying to gray. The gills are usually crowded, brown, attached to nearly free and pallid or grayish, becoming flesh-colored or reddish-pink as the spores mature. The grayish to grayish-brown stalk is longitudinally twisted (hence the species' common name) and covered with silky hairs. The spore print is a deep salmon pink.

Habitat & Season
In woody debris, leaf litter or on rotting logs. Sometimes in grassy areas or on sphagnum moss. April to August.

Brick Top
Naematoloma sublateritium (Hypholoma sublateritium)

Brick Tops appear later in the year than most other fleshy fungi. I've found clusters of them seemingly huddled together for warmth in early December. Caps are convex to nearly plane and brick red, fading to light red or pinkish. The gills are greenish-yellow when young, becoming purple-brown as the spores mature. The white to yellowish stalk is narrow and has a covering of small fibrils. On some specimens, you can see the remnant of a veil toward the top of the stalk. Brick Tops, especially old, faded specimens, can be confused with the poisonous Sulfur Tuft *(Naematoloma fasciculare)* so don't eat this or any other mushroom unless you are 100%, no, 109% certain of your ID. The spores of both species are purple-brown.

A Brick Top doesn't have a brick bottom—the gill color in mature specimens is dark purple-gray or purple-brown.

Habitat & Season
In dense clusters on hardwood logs, stumps and buried debris. August to November, sometimes into December.

Brick Top

Cap: 1–4"

Stem: 2–4"

Aug.–Nov.

Velvet-footed Pax
Paxillus atrotomentosus

In view of its incredibly robust stalk, I'd like to suggest an alternative common name for this species: Big Foot. Often the big foot in question is buried in woody debris, so you might need to dig around if you want to marvel at it.

The hairy cap varies in color from yellow to rust brown, becoming darker and plane in age, but usually retaining an inrolled margin. The entire top skin or cuticle can easily be peeled away from the cap. The dull yellow gills are slightly decurrent, fork near the stalk and sometimes form pores. You can peel them off even more easily than you can peel off the cap cuticle. The "big foot" itself is usually off-center and covered with a dense matting of brown to blackish-brown hairs. If you touch it, you'll swear that you're touching velvet. The spore print is white.

A Case of Rot
The Velvet Foot is one of the fungal species that causes brown rot. If you peer at its substrate, you'll notice that the wood is crumbly, brown and transformed into irregular cubes. Brown rot

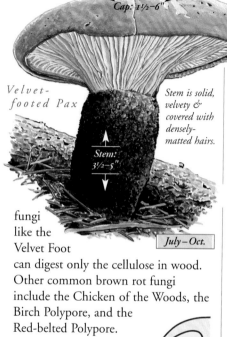

Velvet-footed Pax

Cap: 1½–6"

Stem is solid, velvety & covered with densely-matted hairs.

Stem: 3½–5"

July – Oct.

fungi like the Velvet Foot can digest only the cellulose in wood. Other common brown rot fungi include the Chicken of the Woods, the Birch Polypore, and the Red-belted Polypore.

Dyer's Note
Dye extracts from this mushroom can turn yarns a lovely moss-green color.

Gills: varied length and decurrent. Can form pore-like structures

Habitat & Season
Single or in small clusters on decaying conifer wood. July to October.

Scaly Pholiota
Pholiota squarrosa

If a fungal species is covered with scales, that doesn't make it repulsive. Consider the Scaly Pholiota. Both its cap and stalk are festooned with scales, and it's one of the most attractive mushrooms around. The scales are upright or recurved and much darker than the yellow or buff cap that they decorate. This cap is dry, bell-shaped to nearly flat and often smells like onions. The gills are attached, crowded and pale yellow to yellowish green, becoming brown at maturity. The stalk has a ring that often drops off in age. Above this ring (or ring zone), the stalk is

Cap: 1–5"

Both cap and stem are quite shaggy.

Stem: 2–3"

Scaly Pholiota

smooth, but below it, those lovely scales return. The Sharp-scaly Pholiota (*Pholiota squarrosoides*) is similar, but its cap is slimy beneath the scales. Both species have brown spores.

Habitat & Season

In groups or clusters on living trees, stumps and logs. July to October.

Spore Print

Gills: attached, notched and crowded

Split Gill
Schizophyllum commune

Given the fact that its hyphae have over 25,000 mating combinations, it's not surprising that the Split Gill is perhaps the most widespread fungal species in the world. I've seen it in the Canadian Subarctic as well as the jungles of Borneo. It grows mostly on wood, but it also turns up on bone and human scar tissue.

The caps are hairy, grayish to white and fan-shaped, with an inrolled margin. Since they're attached directly to their substrate, there's no stalk. Nor does the Split Gill have actual gills. Instead, it has pinkish gill-like folds that are seldom more than a millimeter apart. The species derives its name from the fact that these folds look like they've been split by a nano-awl. Spores are white.

Survivor!
To endure hot, cold, or dry conditions, the Split Gill shrivels up. Once conditions improve, it will rehydrate. Specimens have been known to remain shriveled for as long as 50 years, then revive once they've been moistened. Small wonder that the species has succeeded in conquering the world.

Note the very distinctive doubled rows: the "Split gills" are really two adjacent but separate gills.

Cap: 3/8–1 5/8"

Habitat & Season
Scattered or in clusters on hardwood logs and dead hardwood branches. Year-round.

May be the most widespread mushroom in the world.

Year-round

Split Gill

De Gustibus

*S*everal years ago, I found myself in a taxi in Kuching, the largest town in Borneo. The taxi driver, a voluble Malay man, asked me the question that taxi drivers invariably ask foreigners in Kuching: "Want girl?" When I said no, he was undaunted. "Want boy, then?" he inquired. "Sorry, no," I said. "Maybe you want dog? I can arrange." "I want kulat *(mushrooms)!*" I told him.

He looked at me as if I was a pervert, and then drove me to Kuching's Central Market, where I saw huge piles of fruits, vegetables and—one of Borneo's gastronomic specialties—cicadas. Most vendors also had piles of fresh and dried mushrooms, including Boletes, wood ears, Russulas, and Split Gills, a species no guidebook I know describes as edible. Even so, the Split Gill is the most popular edible mushroom in Borneo. However, it's not the Split Gill's flavor or lack thereof that locals crave, but its leathery consistency. After all, this was Asia, where texture and flavor are synonymous.

Later I sampled some Split Gills in a dish of glutinous rice. I have to admit that I found them inferior even to the topping of stewed monkey eye I also ate during my travels in Borneo. That my hosts regarded them as a culinary delight proves once and for all that there is no disputing matters of taste.

Oyster Mushroom
Pleurotus ostreatus

*A*lthough Oyster Mushrooms are frequently grown by home mushroom cultivators, wild specimens, to me, taste much better than their domesticated counterparts. If you go into the wild, you can find this species virtually any time of year, including the winter. Note, however, that the cap in spring or summer is usually white to cream-colored, and that it's much darker—gray to lead-gray to almost brown—later in the year. Likewise, an Oyster Mushroom's cap can be shaped like an oyster shell, a fan or even a funnel. It's also convex to broadly convex, lobed or wavy and often upturned in age. Radiating from the point of attachment, the typically decurrent gills are cream-colored, becoming yellowish or slightly brownish in age. Most Oyster Mushrooms don't have stems, but

Note the gills' wide spacing and the many interspersed shorter gills.

when they do, the stem is short, stout, off-center and covered with tiny hairs. The spore print can be white, buff or pale pink.

A Complex Issue

The Oyster Mushroom is another (yet another!) species complex. The beginning myco-person should simply repeat the following mantra (with apologies to Gertrude Stein): *An Oyster is an Oyster is an Oyster.* On the other hand, there are several look-alike species in New England. *Pleurotus populinus* can be distinguished from *P. ostreatus* by the fact that it grows primarily on aspen and cottonwood, while *P. dryinus* has a membranous veil in the button stage.

Eco-Warrior

Mycologist Paul Stamets has cleaned up several sites contaminated by diesel fuel by inoculating them with the mycelia of Oyster Mushrooms. The species also has been used in straw mats to collect and digest oil spills, including a recent spill off the coast of Spain. How can an Oyster manage such a feat? Its mycelium has the ability to break down polycyclic aromatic hydrocarbons, the core molecules in oil.

Habitat & Season

Single, but more often in large tiers or overlapping masses on dead hardwoods, especially oak. Year-round.

Look who's coming for dinner: Oyster Mushrooms are often home to prolific tiny pleasing fungus beetles (Family Erotylidae) such as Triplax thoracica.

Cap: 2–8"

Stem: if present, up to 1 1/2"

Two forms may be observed. The light-capped ones grow in warmer weather, the dark- or gray-capped ones appear in cooler times.

When growing out of the side of a log, the stem is lateral or absent, but it's more central when atop the log.

Year-round

Spore Print

Attack of the Killer Hyphae!

*T*he dead wood on stumps, trunks and logs is deficient in nitrogen, but invertebrates are not. The Oyster Mushroom is fully aware of this, so it kills and digests the nematodes (tiny roundworms) living in dead wood. Its hyphae secrete droplets of a toxin that paralyzes the unsuspecting nematode, then they seek out the critter's mouth, enter it and munch away at the nitrogen-rich snack from within. To quote mycologist Sam Ristich: "Ain't Ma Nature a crafty Wizardess?"

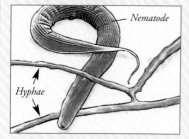

Nematode

Hyphae

Bacteria are also on an Oyster's grocery list. Once the mushroom's hyphae detect a colony of these tasty little morsels, they penetrate that colony and form specialized feeding cells that transport the nutrients back to the main mycelium. In the end, nothing is left of the bacterial colony, not even a memory.

Train Wrecker
Neolentinus lepideus (Lentinus lepideus)

A robust cousin of the shiitake (*Lentinus edodes*), the Train Wrecker has a long life span—specimens well past their prime to seem enjoy flaunting their decrepit, barely identifiable fruiting bodies. Fresh specimens have a tough pale yellow cap with coarse cinnamon to brown scales and an incurved margin when young. Gills are adnate to slightly decurrent, broad and white but aging or bruising yellow-brown, with edges that look like they've been gnawed upon by some small critter. These serrated edges are a diagnostic feature for most mature *Neolentinus*, *Lentinellus* or *Lentinus* species. Usually tapering downward, the stalk is solid, colored like the cap, covered with brownish scales and has a white ring that often disappears in age. Young specimens sometimes smell like anise. The spore print is white.

If it's large, possesses a mushroom shape and is growing on worked wood, then it's probably a Train Wrecker.

Cap: 2 – 10"

The gills have serrated or jagged edges.

May – Sept.

Stem: 2–4"

Fungal Terrorist

This species is called the Train Wrecker because it's been implicated in the brown rot decay of railway ties. Since it will attack any worked timber, you could just as readily call it the Telephone Pole Wrecker or the Fence Post Wrecker. Here's its secret: its mycelium is more or less resistant to creosote as well as other chemicals used to treat wood.

Habitat & Season

Solitary, scattered or in clusters on coniferous wood and sometimes oak. Especially delights in growing on railway ties, fence posts, wooden paving blocks, etc. May to September.

Tree Volvariella
Volvariella bombycina

The Tree Volvariella proves that a mushroom doesn't need to be brightly colored to be striking. It has a white, sometimes quite large conic to convex cap whose coating of fibrils gives a glossy sheen. The gills are crowded, free from the stem, finely fringed and at first white, then pinkish with age. The stalk is smooth, white, firm and either tapered upward or tapered downward. Its piece de resistance is a prominent sac-like or cup-shaped volva at the base of the stem.

V. bombycina can be distinguished from *Amanita* species by its growth on wood and pinkish to brownish spores.

Cap: 2–8"

Stem: 2⅜–8"

July–Oct.

Tree Volvariella

Habitat & Season

Usually solitary or in small groups on dead hardwood trees. Also fruits in the wounds of living hardwoods. July to October.

The Tree Volvariella starts its life in a pronounced sac-like volva.

Gills: spaced and free

Spore Print

Do fungal wonders ever cease? This robust species is a close cousin of the Paddy Straw Mushroom cultivated in the Far East.

Deer Mushroom
Pluteus cervinus

Both the common and scientific name of this species derive from its cap color, which reputedly is the same as a deer. But the fibrillose (furry) cap actually has a far greater range of colors—blackish-brown, cinnamon-brown, light gray, smoky-gray, and in one variety even white—than the range of colors in deer. The gills are free (see insert), more or less crowded and white when young, but pinkish when the spores are mature. The long white stalk is usually covered with grayish or brownish fibers and has no veil. A very common species in New England—as common, in fact, as deer. The spore print is salmon to pink.

Cap: 1–4¾"

Stem: 2–5"

June – Oct.

"Free" gills are not attached to stem

Gills

Stem

Free Gills
This is a good species for observing what mycologists call free gills. Hold a specimen, stem up, in your palm. Note where the stem and cap join in other species. With the Deer Mushroom, they stop before reaching the stem.

Spore Print

Habitat & Season
Solitary or in small clusters on decaying conifers and hardwoods. Sometimes on mulch and sawdust. June to October.

A Sense of Smell

A mushroom's smell can be just as useful as its appearance in helping you to identify it. If you crush a piece of a Deer Mushroom between your fingers, you'll usually detect a radishy odor. Many other mushrooms have equally distinctive smells: Amanita citrina *smells like raw potatoes;* Lactarius hibbardiae *boasts the odor of coconuts; certain* Inocybes *have a spermatic odor;* Marasmius scorodonius *smells like garlic; chanterelles typically smell like fresh apricots; the odor of certain truffles resembles the male sex hormone of pigs; most stinkhorns have the odor of ripe carrion; and so on.*

Then there's the so-called "mushroomy" smell. If a Russula *smells mushroomy, then it's probably not* Russula xeramphalina, *which smells like crab meat; and if a* Tricholoma *smells mushroomy, it's probably not* Tricholoma saponaceum, *which smells like soap. Here I might add that "mushroomy" is an actual smell—the chemical responsible for it has been identified as 1-octen-3-ol. I might also add that you won't get sick or die if you smell a poisonous mushroom. To do that, you would need to get a sizable chunk of that mushroom in your stomach, not just a few of its spores in your nostrils.*

Orange Mock Oyster
Phyllotopsis nidulans

Orange Mock Oyster is not an oyster mushroom, nor does it mock, or in any way ridicule, its fellow wood inhabitors. On the other hand, it may mock the traditional mushroomy smell that so many of us know and love, for specimens growing on hardwoods (but not conifers!) tend to give off an odor that's been variously compared to rotten eggs, rotten cabbage, or methane.

The orange to orange-yellow caps are fan-shaped or kidney-shaped, with an inrolled margin. In age, they become quite hairy; old specimens can be downright hirsute. The close to distant gills are attached to a hairy base (there is no stalk) and remain bright orange well after the cap itself has faded. The spores are pinkish to pinkish-tan.

Habitat & Season
Single or in groups on dead hardwoods and conifers. July to November, but revives during winter thaws.

Orange Mock Oyster

Cap: 1–4"

Specimens on hardwoods smell like methane or rotten eggs!

Look for an inrolled margin and a whitish fuzz.

July – Nov.

Late Fall Oyster
Panellus serotinus

The Late Fall Oyster is not an Oyster Mushroom, but it does fruit in the late fall or even early winter (*serotinus* means "late flowering"). The glutinous layer beneath the cuticle of its cap helps protect it from the cold. That cap itself is smooth and somewhat rubbery, fan or kidney-shaped and viscid when moist. It can be brownish, olive-green, yellow-green or yellowish with purple tints as well as purple with yellowish tints. In my experience, the purple becomes a more dominant color later in its fruiting season. The gills are adnate to decurrent, close and orangish to yellow, becoming paler in age. The stem is short and stubby, scaly or hairy and colored more or less like the cap. The spore print is yellowish.

Habitat & Season
Single or in overlapping clusters on the branches, trunks and logs of dead hardwoods, especially beech and sugar maple. October to December or January.

Late developer—this species doesn't start appearing in New England until October.

Late Fall Oyster

Cap: 1–4"

Stem: less than 1"

Oct. – Jan.

A purple or greenish kidney growing on a log? No, it's probably a Late Fall Oyster.

Broad Gill

Megacollybia platyphylla (Tricholomopsis platyphylla)

Over the years, *Megacollybia platyphylla* has migrated from one genus to another, but its species name has remained the same. At some point it was given a common name—Platterful Mushroom—that sounded like its species name, *platyphylla*. Mistake! For those who decided to eat this mildly toxic species by the platterful ended up with nausea and diarrhea. "Broad Gill" would seem to be a much safer name.

This is among the earliest gilled mushrooms to appear in the spring. The silver-gray to brownish-gray cap is smooth, convex to plane and streaked with dark radial fibers. The gills are attached, distant, very broad (deep) and whitish. The grayish-white to white stalk usually has a bundle of white rhizomorphs at the base. The flesh of the Broad Gill is surprisingly thin and fragile. Spore print is white.

Habitat & Season

Single to scattered on or near rotting deciduous wood. Sometimes on buried wood. May to October.

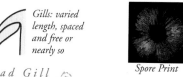

Gills: varied length, spaced and free or nearly so

Spore Print

Broad Gill

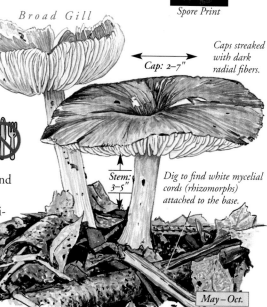

Cap: 2–7"

Caps streaked with dark radial fibers.

Stem: 3–5"

Dig to find white mycelial cords (rhizomorphs) attached to the base.

May – Oct.

Honey Mushroom
Armillaria mellea

Cap: 1–4"

Typical growth habit...in bunches.

Stem: 2–6"

Caps are usually yellow-brown and decorated with blackish hairs, especially in the middle.

July–Nov.

Honey Mushroom

The name Honey Mushroom doesn't refer to this species' flavor, much less its disposition, but to its honey-colored cap. I should say its *sometimes* honey-colored cap, for that cap is often rusty-brown, pinkish, or even soft-red. In fact, there are at least ten different species that commonly go under the name of Honey Mushroom. Several of them are responsible for considerable timber loss in eastern North America (see "Deadly Shoestrings," next page).

Honey Mushrooms typically fruit in large clusters at the base of trees. Their convex, often umbonate caps are covered with short blackish hairs or scales. The usually distant gills are adnate to slightly decurrent and white to cream-colored, developing reddish spots in age. The white or brownish stalk is tough, fibrous and enlarged downward, with delicate scales above a flaring ring and more coarse scales below it.

Honey Mushrooms bear some resemblance to several toxic species, so when in doubt, get a spore print. Actually, they will provide you with a spore print themselves—their white spores often cover the caps of adjoining mushrooms in a cluster.

Gills: decurrent and well-separated

Spore Print

Deadly Shoestrings

Don't think that just because they're called Honey Mushrooms, *Armillaria* species are all sweetness and light. Quite the contrary. They produce a condition in trees and shrubs known as "shoestring rot" or "bootlace rot." This is a root rot, although you might first see evidence of it in the splitting of lower trunk bark and the premature falling of leaves. Shoestring-like cords of hyphae called rhizomorphs travel through the soil until they come in contact with the roots of a potential host, and then they begin digesting that host's wood. The result is a spongy white pulp. You can see these insatiable black rhizomorphs if you peel away the bark on a dead or soon-to-be-dead tree. They look just like black shoestrings, but unlike shoestrings they're coated with a laminate that helps insulate them in cold weather.

Honey Mushroom buttons

The host trees in New England are primarily hardwoods.

Glow-in-the-dark Fungus

Under certain conditions (especially following a good rain), the rhizomorphs or mycelium will glow in the dark, looking quite a bit like skinny skeletal fingers seemingly floating in space.

Habitat & Season

Solitary or more commonly in large clusters at the base of living and dead trees. Sometimes on decaying logs or buried wood. Usually parasitic or saprobic on hardwoods as well as mycorrhizal with several orchid species. July to November.

World's Largest Living Thing

*V*arious species of Armillaria *seem to be competing with each other to be the world's largest living organism. Several years ago, DNA testing indicated that the mycelial mat of a single* Armillaria gallica *inhabited some thirty acres of forest in Michigan's Upper Peninsula. This giant fungus was estimated to be 1,500 years old.*

Then an Armillaria ostoyae *mycelium was discovered in Washington state that extended for 2.5 square miles. But this grandiose organism turned out to be pint-sized compared to an* A. ostoyae *subsequently found in Oregon. Its mycelium covers 3.5 square miles and is estimated to be at least 2,000 years old.*

I suspect that an even larger, not to mention older Armillaria *is currently waiting in the wings to be discovered. Could it be growing in your area?*

Malheur National Forest, Oregon

Night Light
Panellus stipticus

Another bioluminescent species, but in my experience its glow is rather dim compared to a Jack O'Lantern's. Still, we should be grateful for small glows, especially in the winter, a time when the Night Light often fruits. Here let me add that the glow in question is light green, and that it's produced only by the gills, not the entire fruiting body.

The cap is dry, tannish or pale brown, semi-circular to kidney-shaped and minutely hairy. The gills are (not green!) brownish-yellow to cinnamon or even brown, crowded and adnate to slightly decurrent. Colored like the cap or lighter, the stem is often little more than a nub attaching the fruiting body to its substrate.

Night Light gills by day

Although the gills seem to indicate that the spore print will be brown, they're only trying to fool you—the spores are actually white.

Local Chauvinism
Eat your hearts out, denizens of the British Isles. Your *Panellus stipticus* doesn't glow at all, while North American fruiting bodies do. What's more, specimens in the Northeast glow more obviously than specimens in other parts of North America.

The gills of fresh specimens produce a green glow at night.

Stem: 1/8–1/2"

Cap: 1/2–1 1/2"

Year-round

Night Light

Always grows on log or stumps, never on living trees.

A Versatile Fungus

A photographic darkroom is the best place to see the greenish glow of a *P. stipticus*. Let's say you're fumbling around in the dark of a darkroom, and you have happen to cut yourself on a sharp object. Not to worry. The mushroom's species name is derived from its former use as a styptic (blood-clotter), so just apply an infusion from it on your wound, and you'll soon be, if not golden, at least a lot less red.

Habitat & Season

Usually in large numbers or clusters on hardwood logs, branches and stumps. An important saprobe. Year-round.

GILLED
on
OTHER

Most gilled fungi can be found either on the ground or on decaying wood. Most, but not all. *Baeospora myosura* fruits on pinecones, usually the cones of Eastern White Pine; *Marasmius capillaris* fruits on the veins of oak leaves; *Asterophoras* grow on the rotting masses of old *Russula* and *Lactarius* caps; and a number of gilled species find herbivore dung a remarkably congenial substrate.

Remember: if it's organic, then you'll probably find some fungal entity eager to inhabit it. Several years ago, I noticed a discarded, quite old brassiere in a friend's basement. Something about this brassiere caught my eye. Yes, several small Inky Caps were indeed using its frayed fabric as a substrate. You might consider this gross, but then a fungus might think the over-sanitized home environment of most humans is gross, too.

Powder Cap *Asterophora lycoperdoides (Nyctalis asterophora)*

You'll often find clusters of this small parasitic species on *Russulas* and *Lactarius* so rotten that they no longer look like fungi... or anything else. At first you might think they're miniature puffballs, but then you'll see gills, albeit gills that are seemingly unfinished, as if the mushroom was saying, I've decided I don't want gills. Indeed, Powder Caps produce very few spores via their inchoate gills. Instead, special hyphae in the cap discharge thick-walled asexual spores called chlamydospores. These chlamydospores are designed to survive very hot, very cold, or very dry conditions. If you touch a cap, you're likely to get them on your hand, but don't worry: they won't mistake that hand for a rotting *Russula*. Spore print (when obtainable) is white.

Puffballs? Not!

These small mushrooms may be mistaken for puffballs due to their poorly formed gills and rounded cap; but there are no parasitic puffballs.

Mature Powder Caps turn tannish-brown.

Cap up to 1"

Habitat & Season

Few to many on the blackened carcasses of *Russula* and *Lactarius* species. July to November.

The host mushroom is often not this well preserved; it may be an unrecognizable black mass of mush.

July–Nov.

Oak Leaf Marasmius *Marasmius capillaris*

Once upon a time fairies reputedly held nocturnal get-togethers on the caps of Fairy Ring Mushrooms (*Marasmius oreades*), but the far more delicate, indeed more fairylike Oak Leaf Marasmius would seem to be a more likely fairy habitat. On the other hand, a fairy weighing more than a few milligrams would probably crush one of these dainty little mushrooms.

The species emerges after rain on the veins of (primarily) oak leaves. The pleated white to buff cap is umbrella-shaped and has a nub-like umbo. The white gills are attached and distant—a common *Marasmius* feature. The stalk is black, shiny, and tough. Like many other *Marasmius* species, the Oak Leaf Marasmius tends to shrivel up at the drop of a fairy's hat. The spores are white.

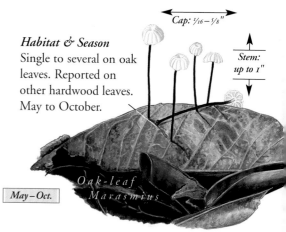

Cap: ⅟₁₆–⅝"

Stem: up to 1"

Habitat & Season
Single to several on oak leaves. Reported on other hardwood leaves. May to October.

May – Oct.

Oak-leaf Marasmius

Conifer-cone Baeospora
Baeospora myosura

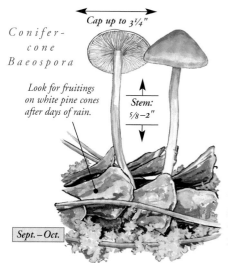

Conifer-cone Baeospora

Cap up to 3¼"

Look for fruitings on white pine cones after days of rain.

Stem: ⅝–2"

Sept. – Oct.

Baeospora myosura inhabits the small world of a single pinecone, specifically the cones of Eastern White Pine and Norway Spruce. The mushroom has a delicate dome-shaped cap with sunken center, smooth moist surface and an inrolled, wavy margin. Cap color is cinnamon or brownish mauve, fading to whitish. The narrow white gills are attached and exceptionally crowded. The hollow, spindly stem is initially white but becomes brownish.

Its dry surface is covered by minute white hairs. Longer hairs at the stem base attach the mushroom to the cone of its choice. Spore print is white.

Habitat & Season
On conifer cones. September and October.

Gills: crowded, varied length and attached

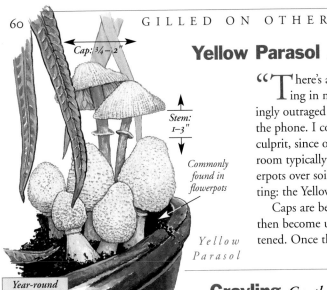

Cap: ¾–2"

Stem: 1–3"

Commonly found in flowerpots

Yellow Parasol

Year-round

Yellow Parasol *Leucocoprinus birnbaumii (Lepiota lutea)*

"There's a yellow mushroom growing in my flowerpot!" the seemingly outraged woman said to me over the phone. I could easily identify the culprit, since only one yellow mushroom typically chooses the soil in flowerpots over soil in a more natural setting: the Yellow Parasol.

Caps are bell-shaped and powdery, then become umbonate and finally flattened. Once the powder starts to fall off, you can see striations on the cap's margin. The gills are free, crowded and often a paler shade of yellow than the cap. The slender stem is dry and powdery, with a collar-like ring that usually disappears in age. The spore print is white.

Habitat & Season
In the potting soil of flowerpots and planter boxes. Sometimes in wood mulch and gardens. Year-round.

Grayling *Cantharellula umbonata*

Formerly classified with chanterelles, the species is neither related to a chanterelle nor to the freshwater fish also called a Grayling. The gray to silver-gray cap is convex, soon becoming flat and depressed at the center with a small pointed umbo. The gills are decurrent, crowded, white to cream-colored and usually forked. When handled or in age, they stain reddish. The stem is off-white to pale gray. Spores are white.

Moss Lover
Graylings fruit in haircap moss (*Polytrichum* sp.) 97.2 percent of the time. They use that moss not only as a substrate, but also as an insulating medium. That's why you tend to find them not only later in the year, but also in cooler weather than most other fleshy fungi.

Habitat & Season
Scattered or in groups in haircap moss. August to late November.

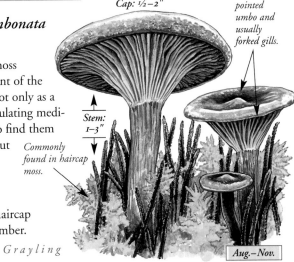

Cap: ½–2"

Note small pointed umbo and usually forked gills.

Stem: 1–3"

Commonly found in haircap moss.

Grayling

Aug.–Nov.

Dung Roundhead
Stropharia semiglobata (Psilocybe semiglobata)

Commonly called Shithead in certain parts of New England because its cap is vaguely headlike, and because it grows only on herbivore dung. The cap is hemispheric when young, smooth, viscid when fresh and pale yellow to yellow. Veil fragments often hang down from its whitish margin. The gills are attached, close to sub-distant and grayish, turning purple-black as the spores mature. The stalk has a fragile ring that tends to fall off in age, leaving a fibrillose zone. Long, slender, and usually slimy, it has the constitution of an acrobat, since it's responsible for the delicate balancing act a Dung Head performs on its excremental substrate. The spore print is dark purple-brown to black.

Habitat & Season
Solitary to several on the dung of deer, moose, horses, cattle, and other herbivores. June to October.

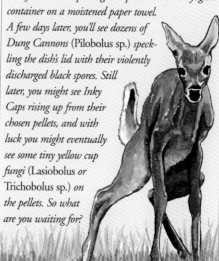

Look for the thin ring that is normally dusted dark from the falling spores.

Cap: 3/8–2"

Stem: 2–6"

Dung Roundhead

Spore Print

Gills: adnate and closely spaced

Grows on the dung of herbivores — cows, horses, white-tailed deer and moose.

June – Oct.

NON-GILLED *on* GROUND

I f a fungal species is growing on the ground, that doesn't necessarily mean it will have gills. Its fertile surface (hymenium) might have pores, teeth, brainlike convolutions, a coral shape, and a lot else. In this section, you'll begin your journey into the varied world of non-gilled fungi. Brace yourself for an exhilarating ride!

First, however, let me qualify the phrase "on the ground." Many species that appear to be growing on the ground are actually growing on buried wood. Such species include puffballs, Dead Man's Fingers, cup fungi and stinkhorns. When it suits them, some of these species will fruit on the ground as well. So in what section do you put them? I've resolved this thorny issue by not resolving it at all. Obvious wood inhabitors are in the next section; not so obvious ones are in this section.

And then there's the chanterelle. It does grow on the ground, but it doesn't have gills radiating down its vaselike fruiting body. Instead, it has gill-like ridges or gill-like folds. This error has been responsible for a vast number of unhappy human stomachs down through the centuries.

Black Trumpet
Craterellus fallax

A lso known as Horn of Plenty, Black Chanterelle and—to the French—*trompette de la mort*. Initially hard to see, but when you see one Black Trumpet, you usually see an entire brass band of them, with dozens of specimens on the ground around you. Fruiting bodies are vaselike or trumpet-shaped, dark gray or black, hollow and brittle, with a margin that's wavy or split in age. The fertile or outside surface is pale gray, decorated with vein-like wrinkles and decurrent almost to the base. Sometimes you can catch a whiff of Black Trumpets before you see them. The odor seems to mingle apricots with perfume from a lady's boudoir. The similar *Craterellus cornucopioides* has a white spore print, while *C. fallax* itself has a light orange to orangish buff spore print.

Habitat & Season
Scattered or in tightly packed clusters with hardwoods. Often found in open places or along trails in the woods. June to October.

Black Trumpet

Cap: 3/8–3"

Fungus: 1–5"

June – Oct.

The Black Trumpet has a fragrant, pleasant odor.

Spore Print

Chanterelle
Cantharellus cibarius

One of the best-known mushrooms in the world as well as one of the most commonly misidentified. True chanterelles have ridges, not gills. These ridges are shallow and thick, fusing and splitting into irregular veins or folds. They extend most or all of the way down the stalk. They're also yellow to orange-yellow or golden orange, the same color as the cap, but they're much less likely to fade than the cap. That cap typically has a depressed center with an inrolled margin that becomes wavy and uplifted with age. The stalk is tapered downward and sometimes stains orange-brown. The spore print is cream-colored or pale yellow, but pinkish in at least one form.

Similar Species, but not Really
The False Chanterelle *(Hygrophoropsis aurantiaca)* has true gills, grows on wood, and has a brownish cap. The Jack O'Lantern *(Omphalotus olearius)* also has true gills and usually grows in tightly packed clusters at the base of tree stumps or on buried roots.

Pricey or Free?
In Europe and America, chanterelles are considered not just a good edible, but also a gourmet edible. Fresh specimens or dried packets of them can be purchased at upscale food markets for similarly upscale prices. But if you know where to look for them, you can get chanterelles for free. And isn't a forest a much more congenial place than a food emporium illuminated by neon?

Habitat & Season
Scattered or in groups. In the southern part of New England, it grows mostly with hardwoods, while in the northern part, it tends to grow more frequently with conifers. July to October.

Funnel or vase shaped

Chanterelle

Cap: 1¼–6"

Stem: 1–4

Not true gills! These blunt and shallow folds form ridges that run down the stalk and resemble gills.

July – Oct.

King Bolete
Boletus edulis

Called *porcini*, *cep*, King Bolete or simply "*edulis*," as in, "You want to know where my *edulis* patch is? Well, it's somewhere between here and the Alaskan border." There are almost as many forms of this species as there are names. In New England, the two forms you're mostly likely to find differ primarily in the shape of their stalks: one has a club-shaped stalk, and the other a more or less straight stalk. Their caps are convex to nearly plane, yellow-brown to reddish-brown or cinnamon, and smooth to slightly wrinkled.

The pore surface is white, becoming greenish-yellow and usually bruising cinnamon-brown (but not blue!). In both forms, the stalk has a distinctive raised netting (reticulum) on its upper part. The stalk on the club-shaped form is sometimes so squat that it actually looks round, perhaps like a *porcino* (piglet) that's eaten not wisely but too well. The spore print is olive-brown.

Look for fine white netting on upper part of stem.

Cap: 3½–10"

Kings in their court. The club-shaped stem suggests that it has dined not wisely but too well at royal banquets

King Bolete

Stem: 1–10"

A Much Prized Species

The King Bolete is a favorite edible mushroom the world over. It's just as popular with insects as it is with humans, so you'll often find half-eaten or maggot-ridden specimens. Don't revile them. After all, both of you share the same taste... and if you're not careful when you clean your King Boletes, you might be sharing the taste of these insects in another, less attractive way.

Habitat & Season

Single or in groups on the ground in woods, especially with conifers. In urban areas, often with Norway Spruce. June to October.

June – Oct.

Spore Print

Sometimes this species is half-buried in duff.

Bitter Bolete
Tylopilus felleus

A King Bolete look-alike that, in the words of mycologist Elio Schaechter, "promises so much and delivers so very little." Unless you happen to like bitter flavors. The cap is convex to nearly flat, dry and pinkish-brown to purplish-brown, becoming totally brown or tan in age. The white pore surface stains brownish and eventually becomes dingy-pink or cinnamon-brown. The pores are relatively large (1-2 per mm). The stalk is often swollen in the middle or club-shaped, with prominent reticulations on the upper part. Unlike the King Bolete, however, these reticulations are pinkish or brownish against a background colored like the cap. Also, the species' bitter flavor will help you distinguish it from a King Bolete. Spores are pinkish-brown to reddish-brown.

Habitat & Season
Single or in groups on the ground in mixed woods. Sometimes on very rotten logs. June to October.

Cap: 2 – 5"

Look for pinkish pores.

Stem: 2–10"

Note pinkish or brownish reticulations.

Bitter Bolete

June – Oct.

The Boletes

When you're looking at a bolete's pores, you're really looking at the visible part of the tubes that contain the species' basidia. You can easily detach these tubes from the cap flesh. Common bolete genera include (in addition to Boletus) Suillus, Tylopilus, Leccinum, and Gyroporus.

The staining reaction of many boletes is an important aid in identifying them. When they're bruised, they'll stain greenish-blue, brown, cinnamon, olive or black. Often this reaction will occur instantly, but just as often it'll take a minute or two. In age or when it's dry, a specimen might not stain at all.

It's been said that boletes are the safest mushroom for the table, but the sickest I've ever been from eating a mushroom came from mistaking a Boletus sensibilis for a Boletus bicolor. The consequence of this mistake? Open sluices at both ends for 48 hours, plus severe cramps. So be as careful with

Bolete pores

boletes as you would with any other fleshy fungi when considering them as edibles.

Painted Suillus
Suillus pictus

Evolution did an excellent job in painting this attractive member of the Bolete family. Conspicuous red to dark-red fibers rest on a dry yellowish cap, a color combination repeated on the stalk. The cap is convex to nearly plane, with a margin that usually has white cottony veil remnants dangling from it. At first an equally cottony veil covers the pore surface, but it disappears as the mushroom matures. The yellow pores are large, angular, and radially arranged. The stalk is thick, enlarged downward, and covered with reddish scales below the veil or veil zones. Spore print is brown.

Habitat & Season
Single to several on the ground with Eastern White Pines. June to October.

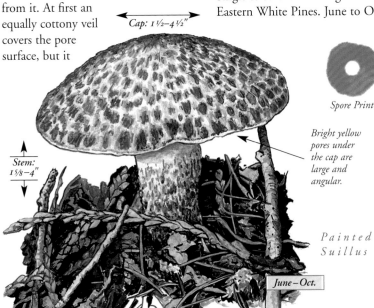

Cap: 1½–4½"

Spore Print

Bright yellow pores under the cap are large and angular.

Stem: 1⅝–4"

Painted Suillus

June–Oct.

Dotted Stalk Suillus
Suillus granulatus

Wherever there are Eastern White Pines in New England, you're likely to find this extremely common species. The cap is convex to flat, slimy or tacky when fresh or wet, and lacks the veil remnants of the Painted Suillus. Its color range is extremely variable— tan, brown, cinnamon, brownish-orange, and dark yellow, although it becomes increasingly cinnamony as it ages. The pores are round to angular and whitish when young, becoming dingy yellow or brownish. The most characteristic feature is the stalk: firm and white or yellowish, it's typically covered from top to bottom with pink to brownish specks known as glandular dots. Sometimes confused with the Chicken Fat Suillus *(Suillus americanus)*, which is much more slimy. Both species have brown spores.

Habitat & Season
Single to several on the ground with conifers, usually Eastern White Pines. Late May to November.

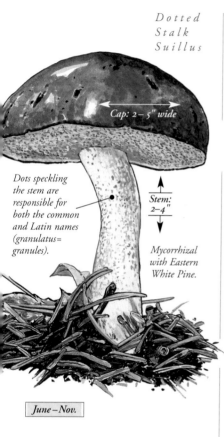

Dotted Stalk Suillus

Cap: 2 – 5" wide

Dots speckling the stem are responsible for both the common and Latin names (granulatus= granules).

Stem: 2–4"

Mycorrhizal with Eastern White Pine.

June – Nov.

Aspen Scaber Stalk
Leccinum insigne

Common all over the Arctic as well as in New England, this bolete has a round cinnamon-orange to brownish cap with a slightly fibrous surface that becomes smooth in age. Pieces of the cap cuticle (outer skin) often hang down from the rim. The white flesh is soft and thick; upon being injured, it first stains lilac-gray, then almost black. Tufts of stiff brown hairs called scabers project from the stem, inspiring Koznyshev, a character in Tolstoy's novel *Anna Karenina*, to say that a *Leccinum's* stem resembles the face of a man who hasn't shaved in two days. I would say four or even five days myself. The spore print is yellowish-brown.

Habitat & Season
Solitary or scattered on the ground under aspen and birch. June or July to October.

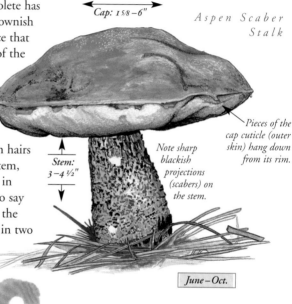

Cap: 1⅝ – 6"

Aspen Scaber Stalk

Pieces of the cap cuticle (outer skin) hang down from its rim.

Stem: 3–4½"

Note sharp blackish projections (scabers) on the stem.

June – Oct.

Spore Print

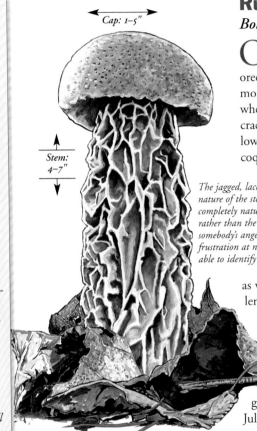

Cap: 1–5"

Stem: 4–7"

The jagged, lacerated nature of the stem is completely natural rather than the result of somebody's anger or frustration at not being able to identify boletes.

July – Sept.

Russell's Bolete

Russell's Bolete
Boletellus russellii

O*ne of the most distinctive of all* boletes. The convex, variously colored (olive-gray, yellow-brown, cinnamon-brown or reddish) cap is smooth when young, but in age becomes cracked, whereupon you can see its yellow flesh peering out in almost a coquettish manner. Neither this flesh or the yellow to greenish-yellow pore surface bruises when cut or rubbed. The stem is the *pièce de résistance* of *Boletellus russellii.* Equal or enlarged downward, it's extremely ragged as well as deeply grooved for its entire length. This makes it look like very shaggy bark or a very shaggy honeycomb. The spore print is dark olive to olive-brown.

Habitat & Season

Single or scattered on the ground under oak, hemlock and pine. July to September.

Red-and-Yellow Bolete
Boletus bicolor

Cap: 2–5"

Red-and-
Yellow
Bolete

Stem:
2–4"

June – Oct.

Here's a conundrum for you: why is this bolete more common than it actually is? The answer: because it's really a complex of several different species, all of which answer to the name of *Boletus bicolor*. Still, these species have several important features in common: a convex to plane dark red cap that becomes yellowish or brown in age; angular, relatively large (1-2 per mm) pores; a yellow pore surface that becomes reddish or olive-tinged and stains greenish-blue or blue slowly (the toxic look-alike *B. sensibilis* stains green or blue right away); and an equal to tapering stalk that's smooth, yellow toward the top and reddish toward the bottom. The stalk may or may not stain greenish or blue, but if it does, it will do so slowly. Slowly = a

The blue-green staining reaction when the stem is cut or bruised can take a minute or two.

minute or two. Spore print is olive-brown.

Habitat & Season
Single, scattered or in groups in the woods or landscaped areas. Associated primarily with oaks, but sometimes grows with aspen. June to October.

Spore Print

Old Man of the Woods
Strobilomyces floccopus

It's hard to confuse this species with any other bolete except perhaps for the aptly named *Strobilomyces confusus*, which looks like it in most respects, but has very stiff scales on its cap. The Old Man of the Woods itself (himself?) has soft to cottony scales that are gray to black-

Cap: 1–6"

Old Man of the Woods

Stem: 1½–5"

July–Oct.

ish against a pale background. The margin of its hemispheric to flattened cap usually has grayish to black veil remnants hanging down from it. The pore surface is white to grayish, becoming black in age. The pores are somewhat angular. The stalk is firm, dry, slightly reticulated at the apex, and covered with soft gray to grayish black scales. All parts stain red, then black when bruised. The spore print is black or blackish-brown.

Spore Print

Dead Men of the Woods
Unlike most other fleshy fungi, the Old Man of the Woods remains intact for quite a long time after releasing its last batch of spores. You often see very old, desiccated specimens still occupying their substrates long after they're no longer viable (i.e., sporulating) members of the fungal community.

Habitat & Season
Single to scattered on the ground in mixed woods. Especially common with oak. June or July to October.

Ash Tree Bolete

Gyrodon merulioides (Boletinellus merulioides)

This curious bolete can be found not only with ash trees, but also with aphids (see "An Admirable Tenant," below). It has a yellow-brown or brown convex to plane cap that often becomes depressed and

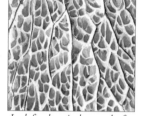

Look for the raised network of crossveins.

wavy in age. The usually decurrent pore surface is yellow, olive-yellow or golden yellow and, instead of conventional pores, it has a raised network of crossveins that sometimes look almost like gills. Colored like the cap, the stalk is decidedly eccentric. This doesn't mean that it behaves like a bachelor uncle in a P. G. Wodehouse novel, but rather that it's off-center. Cap, pores and stalk stain blue or blue-green slowly, then turn reddish-brown. The spore print is olive-brown.

An Admirable Tenant

If you dig up an Ash Tree Bolete, you'll find small black elliptical pellets called sclerotia attached to its mycelium. These sclerotia provide accommodation for aphids feeding off the roots of a nearby ash tree. In lieu of rent, the aphid secretes a sugary "honeydew" on which the mycelium happily dines. Thus this bolete, while associated with ash trees, is not strictly a mycorrhizal species.

Habitat & Season

Scattered or in groups on the group with ash trees. June to October.

Cap: 2–5"

Stem: 1–2"

June – Oct.

Ash Tree Bolete

Sclerotia on the mycelium provide accommodation for aphids, which, instead of rent, secret a honeydrew on which the mycelium feasts.

Morel (Yellow Morel) *Morchella esculenta*

New England cannot boast the abundance of morels commonly found in other parts of the country or in Canada (see "Mush Rush" sidebar). Even so, we do have some morels, and I usually have pretty good luck finding them in old apple orchards. I've also found batches of them in manicured areas next to shopping malls!

Morels are ascomycetes. Think of them as (in the words of mycologist Roy Watling) "a bunch of cup fungi aggregated onto a stalk to form a honeycomb-like structure." These cups, or pits, are highly irregular in size and shape. They form a conical, pinecone-shaped, oval or roundish fruiting body whose color can be yellow, yellow-brown or caramel-brown. The stem is off-white to buff, minutely hairy and hollow. Occasionally, this stem can be so large that it threatens to overwhelm the rest of the fruiting body.

There's usually a single hollow chamber inside the cap.

The difference between the "true" morel and the False Morel (*Gyromitra esculenta*) is more obvious when you cut open the two species—the cap of the actual morel consists of a single hollow chamber, while the cap of the False Morel is multi-chambered. Of course, "true" and "false" are relative terms here. I'm sure the mycelia of both species believe they're the true ones.

Don't be a Sicko!
In a famous incident, a chef put raw morels in the salad at a Royal Canadian Mounted Police convention, and dozens of Mounties ended up with nausea and diarrhea. Be forewarned: while cooked morels are a culinary delicacy, uncooked ones can be a rather indelicate matter for the person who consumes them.

Habitat & Season
In apple orchards, under dying elms or old ash trees and in burnt areas. Usually with hardwoods, but occasionally with conifers (particularly in northern New England). April to early June.

Cap: 1–4½"

Stem: 1–5"

Morel

April – June

Mush Rush

Let's leave New England briefly and travel to Canada's Yukon Territory, where a thousand or more square miles of forest goes up in flames annually. This delights mushroom pickers, for forest fires accelerate the growth of morels. Something about fire-related nutrients or disruptions in the soil causes a morel's mycelium to send up biblical numbers of fruiting bodies, but even mycologists who've studied this phenomenon are not exactly sure why.

The year after a fire, the Yukon is the fungal equivalent of the Gold Rush, with terms like "mother lode" and "bonanza" commonly used to describe large morel fruitings. If you hang around the buying depots, you'll meet charcoal-covered pickers with Gold Rush names like Klondike Mike and Ivan the Terrible. Even before you meet them, you can smell their aroma, a pungent mix of burnt forest, bug dope, sweat and mushrooms.

In all probability, the Yukon's forest fires are the consequence of global warming. New England has yet to see such rampaging fires as well as the accompanying bounty of morels, but stay tuned. It could only be a matter of time…

False Morel (Brain Fungus) *Gyromitra esculenta*

The False Morel bears a certain resemblance to a brain on a stalk. "Cerebriform," in fact, is the scientific term for its lobed, convoluted cap, which (unlike a morel's cap) is divided up into several chambers inside. The thick stem is pallid to buff with a smooth, slightly grooved surface and an enlarged base. Its interior is stuffed with cottony fibrils, two-chambered or hollow. Like the morel, this is exclusively a spring mushroom.

Rocket Fuel Propellant or Gourmet Edible?

Especially in Europe, people claim to eat *G. esculenta* without any ill effect. In Finland, for instance, it recently ranked #6 among the best edible mushrooms. However, the species contains a toxin, monomethylhydrazine (MMH), which is used as a propellant for rocket fuel.

The unpleasant symptoms of MMH occur two to twelve hours after eating. These symptoms include headache, abdominal pain, cramps, diarrhea and vomiting. In severe cases, damage occurs to the liver, kidney and red blood cells. Fourteen percent of reported poisonings have been fatal. But even if you don't get sick at first, the

Cap:
2–4" wide, 1–4" high

Conifer False Morel

Stem:
1–4"

Fruiting body is folded and wrinkled like a brain. One of its common names is the Brain Fungus.

The False Morel's cap is not attached to the stalk except at the very top.

April–June

toxins are cumulative and may be fatal over time. As mycologist David Arora puts it, *"There is a narrow threshold between the amount of MMH the human body can safely absorb and the amount which can cause acute illness, even death. It seems foolhardy to risk eating a mushroom species containing MMH."*

Habitat & Season
Single or scattered on the ground under conifers. Often in yards. April to June.

White Elfin Saddle (White Helvella) *Helvella crispa*

The three-lobed, saddle-shaped cap makes this species relatively easy to identify. At first it might look like a cup fungus with an incurved margin, but in maturity it takes on its distinctive saddle-shaped appearance. The cap is attached to a ribbed stalk in such a seemingly random manner that it looks like it might fall off at any moment. The entire fruiting body is creamy-white, with hints of yellow or pink. When it's growing on wood, *Helvella crispa* is a saprobe, but when it's growing on the ground, it's probably a mycorrhizal species. The spore print is white.

Habitat & Season
Single or in groups in hardwood and coniferous forests. Also on moss-covered rotting wood. June to early November.

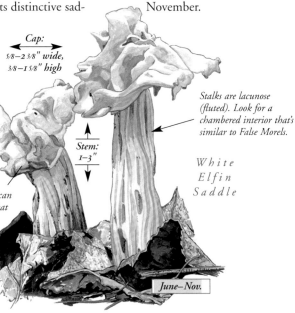

Cap:
5/8–2 3/8" wide, 3/8–1 5/8" high

Stalks are lacunose (fluted). Look for a chambered interior that's similar to False Morels.

Stem: 1–3"

The cap's underside can be somewhat fuzzy.

White Elfin Saddle

June–Nov.

Fairy Stool *Coltricia cinnamomea*

This ground-inhabiting species belongs to the only genus of mycorrhizal polypores, so instead of digesting its host, it forms a mutualistic relationship with it. Its shiny cap is more or less circular, concentrically zoned, bright reddish cinnamon to amber brown, and often centrally depressed. The margin is sometimes torn in age. The pore surface is yellowish-brown to reddish-brown, with irregularly shaped or angular pores. The tough stalk is the same color as the cap and sometimes bent at a crooked angle. Sometimes, too, you'll encounter several specimens fused together to form what might be called a Fairy Sofa.

Habitat & Season
Single to several along well-used trails and in clearings. June to November.

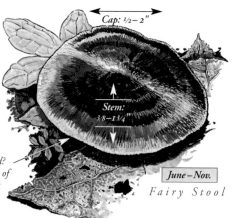

Cap: ½–2"

Stem: 3⁄8–1¾"

June–Nov.

Fairy Stool

A polypore with a stem growing out of the ground? Yes, the Fairy Stool is one of several polypores with this fruiting habit.

Wooly Velvet Polypore *Onnia tomentosa (Inonotus tomentosus)*

Although this polypore would appear to be growing on the ground, it's a root pathogen that causes white pocket rot in its host tree, so it's really growing on buried wood. The cap is circular to semi-circular, more or less velvety in texture, yellow-brown to brown and convex to centrally depressed, with concentric zones. Pores are brown and angular, but sometimes become elongated or even toothlike in age. The stalk (when present) is rudimentary, off-center to lateral, and the same color as the cap. As it grows, the Wooly Velvet Polypore tends to encompass everything in its path, so you'll find specimens with grass, twigs, and pine needled imbedded in them (see insert illustration). I once saw a Bic lighter stuck in the cap of one specimen.

Habitat & Season
Single or in groups on the ground with conifers. August to October or November.

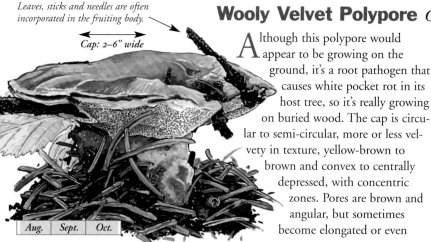

Leaves, sticks and needles are often incorporated in the fruiting body.

Cap: 2–6" wide

| Aug. | Sept. | Oct. |

Sweet Tooth (Hedgehog Mushroom)
Hydnum repandum

Probably the most commonly encountered tooth fungus in New England. The smooth, convex to broadly convex cap is orangish, pale cinnamon or buff, although it's virtually white in one variety. Wavy and indented in age, the Sweet Tooth some-

Cap: 1–6"

times suggests a chanterelle, albeit a chanterelle with teeth. Those teeth are soft, brittle and either cream-colored, pale-orange or orange-brown. The stalk is usually off-center, firm and somewhat lighter in color than the cap. All parts stain yellow or orange-yellow when bruised. *Hydnum umbilicatum* is a similar, but much smaller species with a more deeply sunken center.

Sweet Tooth produces spores on the outside of the tooth-like spines, or "teeth."

Why Teeth?
Every fungal species has a strategy for increased spore production. With tooth fungi, that strategy is an elongated tooth or spinelike structure instead of gills or pores. The point (so to speak) of such structures is not to bite enemy organisms, but to manufacture as many spores as possible.

Habitat and Season
Single to numerous under hardwoods and conifers. More likely under conifers in the northern part of New England. July to November.

Spines recede as they begin to descend the stem, soon disappearing.

Sweet Tooth

Stem: 1–4"

July –Nov.

Bleeding Tooth *Hydnellum peckii*

The Bleeding Tooth doesn't have a bad dental problem, nor is it the victim of a bad dentist. Its fruiting body is exuding reddish droplets of water, a process called guttation. Mycologists aren't really sure why certain fungi guttate. It's possible that they're getting rid of excess water during very wet periods or periods of rapid growth so that they won't become too soggy to drop their spores.

The Bleeding Tooth's cap is white to pinkish, becoming brown and fretted with ridges or projections in age. Only fresh, actively growing specimens have caps that "bleed." The decurrent teeth are pinkish with white tips, but turn brown or purplish-brown in age. The stalk is tough, velvety and colored like the cap. The species has a very acrid or peppery flavor.

Habitat and Season
On the ground with conifers. More common in northern New England. July to October.

An unusual dye—terphenylquinone—is responsible for the red color on this species' droplets.

Cap: 1–6"

Stem: 1–3"

Sept. – Oct.

Bleeding Tooth

The "teeth," which are often hidden beneath the irregular cap, extend down the stalk.

Common Fiber Vase *Thelephora terrestris*

Wrinkled, warty or smooth, its fertile surface tries to touch all bases.

Cap: 1–5"

July – Oct.

Long after they've done their spore-dispersing work on earth, the blackened corpses of *Thelephora terrestris* haunt their former substrates. You might describe them as the zombies of the fungal world.

When fresh, the caps are vase or funnel-shaped, concentrically zoned, brownish, smooth or slightly hairy and usually with a ragged margin. The fertile surface is colored like the cap and smooth except for small warts and occasional wrinkles. A growing *T. terrestris* will absorb anything in its path, including other *T. terrestris* specimens. Indeed, you often see several of them fused together in rosettes or overlapping clusters. Another *Thelephora, T. palmata*, is more coralloid in form and smells like garlic gone bad. Both species are mycorrhizal.

Habitat and Season
Single or in overlapping clusters on the ground with conifers. Especially common in sandy soil. July to November.

Yellow-headed & Green-headed Jelly Babies
Leotia lubrica & Leotia viscosa

These are not different kinds of candy or horror movie newborns, but two closely related species of club fungi. The Yellow-headed Jelly Baby is viscid, with an irregularly round or convoluted head and an inrolled margin. The similarly colored stalk is also viscid, enlarged downward and either hollow or filled with a gel. The Green-headed Jelly Baby differs from its sibling in having, not surprisingly, a green head. It's also con-

Cap: ¼–¾"

Spores are produced on the "baby's" cap surface.

Stem: ¾–1¾"

Green-headed Jelly Baby

siderably less viscid. Other features are more or less the same. Both species are ascomycetes and, in all probability, saprobes.

Habitat and Season
In groups or dense clusters on the ground or rotten woods. Often found in mosses. June to October.

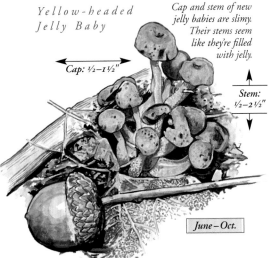

Yellow-headed Jelly Baby

Cap and stem of new jelly babies are slimy. Their stems seem like they're filled with jelly.

Cap: ½–1½"

Stem: ½–2½"

June – Oct.

Jellied False Coral
Tremellodendron pallidum

Composed of numerous broadly flattened to more or less round branches whose tips are often fused. The coral-like fruiting bodies are white to buff, tough and leathery. Often classified with jelly fungi rather than corals not because specimens are gelatinous (truth to tell, they're only slightly gelatinous), but because their basidia are quite similar to those of jellies. Sometimes greenish due to algal growth on the branches. Also called *T. schweinitzii*.

Habitat and Season
On the ground with hardwoods.

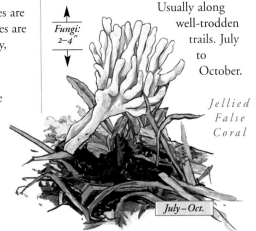

Usually along well-trodden trails. July to October.

Fungi: 2–4"

Jellied False Coral

July – Oct.

Dead Man's Fingers
Xylaria longipes

Dead Man's (but why not Dead Woman's?) Fingers assume different guises during different times of the year. In the spring, the young fruiting bodies are covered with a whitish or gray powder, which isn't really powder but asexual spores. As the spores disperse, the fungus starts turning black, and by early fall it's completely black. Each "finger" is spindle or club-shaped, wrinkled or roughened and occasionally cracked, with a short cylindrical stalk. In maturity, the surface is covered with pimples—not acne, but tiny flasks (perithecia) with asci in them. If you cut open a specimen, you'll see the imbedded parts of these flasks surrounded by white, fibrous flesh. According to Xylariologist Jack Rogers, the species most likely to be found in New England is not *Xylaria polymorpha*, as is commonly thought, but *X. longipes*.

Crime Aid?
Certain African tribes believe that if you've committed a crime, and you rub the spore powder from an immature *Xylaria* on your skin, the police won't identify you as the culprit.

Habitat and Season
Usually clustered on or around hardwood stumps. Often on buried hardwood debris as well. May to early November.

Spores are produced on small flasklike organs that pierce the outer crust of the fungus.

Fungus: 3/4 –3 1/4"

Dead Man's Fingers start out more whitish but turn darker later in the season.

1/2" wide

May – Nov.

Dead Man's Fingers

Velvety Fairy Fan
Spathularia velutipes

3/4–1 3/4" tall

Head: 1/2 – 1 1/2"

The whimsical design of this species is reminiscent of a lady's hand fan that's perhaps seen better days. The fan-like head is yellow or yellowish-brown, folded or wrinkled and sometimes lobed. Its outer edges run down the stalk on opposite sides. The stalk itself, which is akin to the fan's handle, is velvety-brown to bay-brown and usually tapered, with orange mycelial threads at the base. A similar species, *Spathularia flavida*, has a more pallid head and a whitish to yellowish stalk with yellow mycelial threads at the base.

Habitat and Season
In clusters on rotting hardwood logs. Sometimes on the ground with pine. July to September.

Swamp Beacon
Mitrula elegans

A muddy puddle behind a shopping mall wouldn't seem like a very good place to find fungi, but that's where I once found a large fruiting of Swamp Beacons. They seemed to be grinning up at me and saying, "Don't rule out any substrate for us fungi." But muddy puddles aren't the only place where you can find this species. Any moderately wet habitat will do—a swamp, a swale, a ditch, a vernal pool, or even very wet leaves. The fruiting bodies have a pallid to orange head that's usually pear-shaped or spathulate. The stalk is white, pink-tinged or sometimes greenish-tinged, enlarging toward the base. Let me add that Swamp Beacons don't actually grin, but if the light is exactly right, they do seem to glow, which explains how they got their name. Exclusively a spring or early summer species.

Habitat and Season
In large numbers in wet areas. Probably associated with oak or maple leaves. April to July.

Head: ⅛–1 ⅜"

Stem: ½–1¾"

Look for clusters of Swamp Beacon in wet areas.

Aug.–Sept.

Swamp Beacon

Purple Coral
Clavaria zollingeri

When you first see this species, you might wonder if you're hallucinating. Certainly, it's among the most colorful of all coral fungi. The fruiting bodies are deep purple, magenta or lilac-purple, whitish at the base and sparingly or profusely branched. The branch tips are pointed or round, while the branches themselves

1–5"

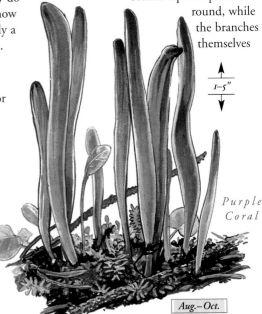

Purple Coral

Aug.–Oct.

are cylindrical and very brittle. The Purple Coral often tastes like radishes (as with all taste tests, a tiny piece on your tongue is sufficient). Similar species include *Alloclavaria purpurea*, which is unbranched, and *Clavulina amethystina*, which typically has more branches as well as no discernible flavor.

Habitat and Season
Usually in groups or dense clusters in mixed woods. Sometimes growing in moss. July to October.

A Short Note on Coral Fungi

Although they're usually lumped together in field guides, corals can be branched, unbranched, club-shaped, worm-shaped, solitary, clustered, tough, easily broken, fused at the base, not fused at the base, edible, poisonous, basidiomycetes, ascomycetes, saprobic, or mycorrhizal. What, you might ask, do corals have in common? Well, all of them look like coral... except those that don't. Welcome to the wonderful world of mycology!

Golden Spindle
Clavulinopsis fusiformis

Golden Spindles look like a group of bright yellow to orange-yellow exclamation points rising up from the ground.

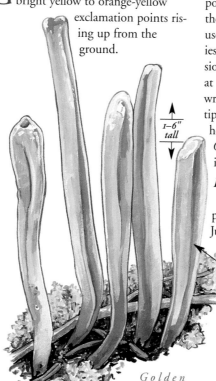

1–6" tall

Golden Spindle

July – Oct.

Or a veritable army of exclamation points: I once saw perhaps a hundred of them exclaiming together along a well-used trail in Connecticut. Fruiting bodies are usually branched, but you occasionally see two or three mini-branches at the apex of specimens. The surface is wrinkled or grooved, with a rounded tip. The usually fleshy interior becomes hollow in age. A similar species, *Clavulinopsis laeticolor*, is more golden in color and smaller in size.

Habitat and Season
In dense clusters in grass, along paths and in the woods, and in moss. July to October.

Look for a groove down the side.

If you find one Golden Spindle, you'll find a whole spindly mass of them.

Black Earth Tongue
Trichoglossum farlowii

1–2½"

Note tiny hairs on surface.

July – Oct.

When you first encounter this species, you might think the earth is sticking out a blackened tongue at you, but that's not the case. Earth Tongues are tongue or lance-shaped saprobic fungi that grow on rotten wood, humus and especially moss. This particular species was named for the eminent Harvard botanist William Gibson Farlow. Its irregularly folded head (please note that W. G. Farlow did not have an irregularly folded head) is so minutely hairy that you'll probably need a hand lens to see the hairs. The stalk is often twisted or curved, longitudinally furrowed and hairy like the head. Actually, the hairs are pointed sterile cells called setae. To identify most Earth Tongue species, you'll need a microscope, since they can be distinguished only by differences in their needle-like spores.

Black Earth Tongue spores

Habitat and Season
On moss, particularly sphagnum moss. Also on rotting wood in wet or swampy areas. July to October.

Irregular Earth Tongue *Neolecta irregularis*

Grows in coniferous forests.

½–3½"

July – Dec.

If Black Earth Tongue suggests that the earth is sticking out a black tongue at you, then this species seems to suggest that the tongue in question is bright orange or bright yellow-orange. Like the Black Earth Tongue, the Irregular Earth Tongue is club or spoon-shaped, but it's much more contorted and compressed—i.e., irregular. It often has a tapering, stalk-like base that's either whitish or pale yellow. The species is usually found at altitudes of 800 feet or more in southern or central New England, but at sea level in northern New England. Another orange Earth Tongue, *Microglossum rufum*, has a much less irregular shape.

Habitat and Season
Scattered to numerous on the ground under conifers. Often found growing on moss. July to November or early December.

Stinkhorns

Those species commonly known as stinkhorns have always inspired a bad press. First, there's their shape, which is highly suggestive. In Victorian England, male servants rose before dawn to rid an estate of these dreaded fungal excrescences, lest they corrupt the morals of the maids. Then there's the smell, which has been compared to ripe carrion. A stinkhorn brought into a room will inspire a collective look of disgust among those people in the room. But a stinkhorn's smell didn't evolve to drive away humans. It exists to attract insects, who either ingest the spores or get them on their feet. Whereupon they become excellent vectors of spore dispersal.

Dog Stinkhorn

Since this is a book about New England fungi, I should mention that in Massachusetts stinkhorns were once called "death babies." If one of them fruited near your house, it was an indication that someone in your family was going to die.

Common Stinkhorn (Ravenel's Stinkhorn)
Phallus ravenelii

Lots of people have *Phalluses* growing in their gardens. Rather than the male organ of generation, I'm talking about *Phallus ravenelii*, New England's most common stinkhorn. Still, the genus name does have a certain appropriateness. A mycologist who'd recently had a newly discovered species named after him wasn't sure that he appreciated having his name affixed to perhaps the smallest known *Phallus*...

Phallus ravenelii grows out of a compressed, embryonic form of itself called an egg. A broken remnant of this egg survives as a cuplike sac or volva at the base of the stalk. The head is covered with a slimy greenish spore mass (gleba) and has an open whitish depression at the top. The stalk is white, hollow and looks like foam rubber. The odor is strong and can be detected at quite a distance. I don't find this odor

Head: 3/4–1 3/4"

Attention all insects! The delightfully fetid spore slime on the heads of fresh specimens is there just for you!

unpleasant, but then I don't find the scent of skunks unpleasant, either.

Stem: 3–6"

Habitat and Season
Solitary to clustered on woody debris and decaying logs or stumps. Frequently in urban and suburban areas. July to early November.

Common Stinkhorn

July–Nov.

Veiled Stinkhorn
Phallus duplicatus (Dictyophora duplicata)

Like other stinkhorns, this arcane species emerges from a puffball-like underground "egg." The bell-shaped, pitted head is coated with a highly odiferous greenish-brown or olive green spore slime (gleba) that eventually falls off or is carried off by insects. The stalk is white, often curved and very spongy. The lacelike veil (indusium) unfurls from the head and often descends to the ground. Flying insects have no problem getting to this species' gleba, but the veil would seem to provide a ladder for non-flying insects who might otherwise have a hard time reaching their destination. Also called the Bridal Veil Stinkhorn, but not recommended for prospective brides unless they want their grooms to annul the marriage.

Habitat and Season
Solitary or in small groups in mixed woods. Frequently in wood chips. June to October.

Head: 1¼–3"

This is the only fungal species with a netlike veil.

3–7"

June – Oct.

Veiled Stinkhorn

Stinky Squid
Pseudocolus schellenbergii

The Stinky Squid looks remarkably like a cephalopod that decided to relocate to an utterly inappropriate habitat—a terrestrial mulch bed.

Head & Arms: 1–3"

The "arms" are often fused at the tip.

The Stinky Squid's spores reside in its dark green gleba.

Stinkhorns hatch from underground, puffball-like eggs.

June – Oct.

Developing from an oval or pear-shaped egg, the fruit body consists of three to six arms and a stalk with a grayish volva. The arms are light yellow to reddish-orange, pitted, curved and covered with a fetid greenish gleba along half to two-thirds of their length. More often than not, they're fused at the tips. The whitish stalk is spongy, somewhat shorter than the arms and attached to the ground by one or more thick white rhizomorphs. First sighted in Pittsburgh in 1915, the Stinky Squid is probably a non-native species brought to the eastern U. S. on imported wood mulch. Also called *Pseudocolus fusiformis*.

Habitat and Season
Saprobic on wood chips, mulch, and rich humus. Commonly found in landscaped areas and on well-used trails. June or July to October.

*Stinky
Squid*

Pear-shaped Puffball
Lycoperdon pyriforme

What witty folks taxonomists are! They decided to call a well-represented puffball genus *Lycoperdon*, which means, "wolf fart" in Latin. I've never been near a flatulent wolf, but I suspect that it's considerably less fun than watching *Lycoperdon* spores explode into the air. The pear-shaped spore case of this species is yellow to yellowish-brown and covered with tiny granules. The spore mass inside the case is white, then becomes yellow and then yellowish-brown when the spores are mature. White rhizomorphs radiating from the tapered, stalkless base help distinguish the Pear-shaped Puffball from other *Lycoperdon* species.

A word of caution: just as you probably shouldn't inhale wolf farts, it's not a good idea to inhale the spores of this or any other puffball. If you inhale too many, you could end up with pulmonary problems.

Habitat and Season
Scattered or in dense clusters on well-rotted wood, especially stumps and logs. July to November.

Head: 1/2–2"

Young puffball

*Mature puffballs:
Note split in skin
prior to release
of spores.*

*Airborne
spores*

With Stem:
3/8–1 3/4"

July–Nov.

*Pear-
shaped
Puffball*

Devil's Snuffbox (Gem-studded Puffball)

Lycoperdon perlatum

Similar to the Pear-shaped Puffball, except that the spore case is covered with cone-shaped spines that earn the species its alternative name, Gem-studded Puffball. Eventually, these spines either fall off or are washed off by rain, leaving a pattern of reticulate scars in their wake. The spore case is whitish at first, then yellowish-brown and then olive-brown, whereas the Pear-shaped Puffball is somewhat darker. The spore mass is firm and white, but becomes powdery and brownish when the spores mature. This species has a large, stalklike base. Probably the most common puffball in New England.

Habitat and Season
Scattered or in groups on mulch, compost piles and rotting logs. Also on the ground in mixed woods. July to November.

Note cream-white interior of a young specimen.

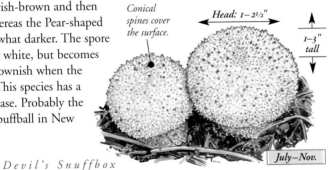

Conical spines cover the surface.

Head: 1–2½"

1–3" tall

July–Nov.

Devil's Snuffbox

Pigskin Poison Puffball (Earthball)

Scleroderma citrinum

The outer rind or peridium of this species does in fact feel like pigskin or a football (historical note: footballs used to be made of pigs' bladders, not pigskin). That peridium is spherical, yellow-brown, relatively thick and covered with small scales or warts. The spore mass is gray to purple, turning purple-black, then black when the spores are mature. The species has a rudimentary stalk with mycelial strands,

Dark spores inside the fruitbody are characteristic of this species.

Poof!

In young edible puffballs, the spore mass inside is firm and white.

A puffball could be mistaken for a golf ball, except that golf balls don't usually sporulate. Most puffballs have a peridium (outer case) that serves as a domicile for the spores. As these spores mature, they become a powdery mass. Once the peridium at the apex breaks open, a raindrop, a scampering chipmunk, or your poking finger will release millions of spores in a tiny cloud that puts the "puff" in a puffball. Whereupon the wind will distribute these spores.

Typical puffball spores

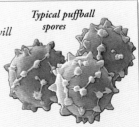

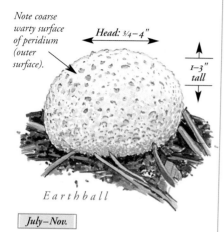

Note coarse warty surface of peridium (outer surface).

Head: ¾–4"

1–3" tall

Earthball

July–Nov.

but you often need to dig into the ground to find it. Sometimes parasitized by a bolete *(Boletus parasiticus)*. You shouldn't eat a Pigskin Poison Puffball unless the prospect of vomiting, nausea and diarrhea appeals to you.

Habitat and Season
Single to several on the ground or on decaying wood. Often on sandy or disturbed soil. July to November.

Barometer Earthstar
Astraeus hygrometricus

When it's young, this species could be confused with a young puffball, perhaps of the Pigskin Poison variety. It starts out as a somewhat flattened off-white to brownish spore sac with a rough warty surface. Inside that sac, there's the usual spore mass that becomes brown and powdery as the spores mature. But it's what happens to the spore sac itself that makes the Barometer Earthstar such a distinctive species—it splits into 6-12 black-gray rays, each decorated with a pattern of cracks. This permits the

Barometer Earthstar

fruiting body to respond acrobatically to changes in the weather. In dry weather, the rays close protectively over the spore sac, but on wet days they spring open... and not just spring open, but also lift up the spore sac so that it can disperse its spores more easily. The Barometer Earth's ability to open and close can go on for quite a long time. A specimen I collected almost ten years ago still opens its rays when I immerse it in a bowl of water.

Habitat and Season
Solitary or scattered in poor or sandy soil. Also in dry open woodlands. More common in Cape Cod than other parts of New England. Year-round.

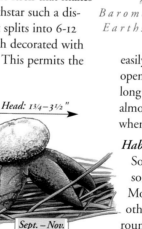

Why a "barometer?" Because the rays open in wet or humid conditions.

Head: 1¾–3½"

Sept. – Nov.

Fruiting body may last all year

Stalked Puffball in Aspic
Calostoma cinnabarina

Young specimens of *Calostoma cinnabarina* look like masses of cherry jelly, but once the stalk elongates to reveal an apical spore sac, you realize that you're seeing an extremely unusual fungus rather than the leavings from a picnic. Gelatinous and bright red, this spore sac has an even more brightly red peristome (spore opening) with seemingly puckered lips—hence the species' alternative name Hot Lips. The interior of the spore sac is white and solid when young, then powdery and buff-colored when the spores are mature. The stalk is spongy, gelatinous and reddish-orange to reddish-brown with netlike reticulations. At first you might think *C. cinnabarina* is some kind of stinkhorn, but its powdery spores and lack of aroma will set you straight. More common in southern New England.

Habitat and Season
Single or numerous in the woods, especially in sandy soil. Also found in moss beds along streams. Mycorrhizal. June or early July to October.

July – Oct.

Stem: 5/8–1 2/3"

3/8–1" wide

Mycologist Elio Schaechter gave this species its alternative common name—"Hot Lips."

Stalked Puffball in Aspic

The stem is like gelatin or aspic.

Splash Cup
Cyathus striatus

Certain members of the Gasteromycete (puffball) family resemble miniature birds' nests replete with eggs. Not surprisingly, they're called Bird's Nest Fungi. There are several common species in New England, but the Splash Cup is perhaps the most

Cups: 1/4–1/3"

July – Nov.

Cups: 1/4–1/3"

Splash Cup

Peridioles (spore sacs) are like eggs in a nest.

common. The name refers to its highly imaginative way of launching its spores. A raindrop strikes one or more of its eggs (peridioles) and sends it flying through the air with a slinky-like device (funiculus) unfurling behind it. A sticky bit at the end of the funiculus wraps around a branch or twig, putting the peridiole in a good position to sporulate.

The Splash Cup's fruiting body is vase-shaped, grayish-brown and covered with tufts of hair. The inner part of the cup is strongly grooved. Eggs are often triangular or irregular in shape and dark gray. Before a raindrop ruptures it, the fruiting body has a whitish lid (epiphragm) with an inrolled margin.

Habitat and Season
Scattered or in dense groups on wood chips, bark, branches and other types of woody debris. July to November.

Orange Peel
Aleuria aurantia

This species looks like a cast-off orange peel, especially since it's usually found in the same sorts of disturbed areas where you find cast-off orange peels. The fruiting body is cup-shaped when young, but becomes less and less cup-shaped as it ages and also develops a wavy, irregular margin. The thin flesh is so brittle that if it were a person, Tennessee Williams would have been obliged to write a play about it. The outer surface is a pale yellow-orange, while the inner surface is bright orange.

A Cause for Celebration
Approximately, 99.9 percent of all Orange Peels are orange, but rare albino (all-white) forms do exist. If you're so lucky as to find a white specimen, you should dance up and down with excitement!

Habitat and Season
In groups or clusters on paths, along roadsides, and in open woodlands. Especially common on loamy siliceous ground. June to November.

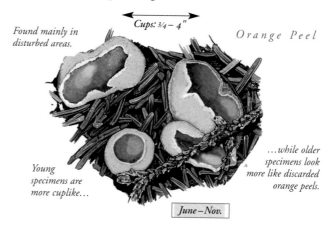

Found mainly in disturbed areas.

Cups: ¾ – 4"

Orange Peel

Young specimens are more cuplike…

…while older specimens look more like discarded orange peels.

June – Nov.

NON-GILLED on WOOD

Due to the decline of both farming and logging, there are now more trees in New England than there were 150 years ago. This means that there are more logs and more rotten wood, too. If you're a wood-inhabiting fungus, you might feel that you've gone from famine to feast.

Among non-gilled wood-inhabitors, polypores are the most obvious. That's because they tend to live longer and they're bigger than other fungi. Here's an instructive comparison: the fruiting body of a chanterelle has a life expectancy of less than a week, while an Artist's Conk can live almost as long as a human.

Other non-gilled species that find wood a congenial substrate include jellies, cup or sac fungi, crust fungi and a number of toothed (hydnaceous) fungi.

Wood-inhabiting species can be described as either predecessors or successors: a successor can't eat until a predecessor has eaten first and tempered the wood for it. On the other hand, some wood-inhabiting species—like certain jellies—do not digest wood, but rather dine on the mycelia of other species.

Jelly Tooth
Pseudohydnum gelatinosum

Called *Pseudohydnum gelatinosum* because, unlike other toothed species, it happens to be a jelly fungus. Caps are rubbery, tongue, spoon or fan-shaped, slightly hairy or smooth, and translucent white to gray or even slightly bluish in color. As if it was a bit self-conscious about having teeth, the projections on the cap's underside are more like nubs or warts than actual teeth. Some specimens have a translucent grayish stalk, while others do not. Those that lack a stalk may in fact be a wholly different species.

The teeth on this unusual species—the only toothed jelly—usually look less like teeth and more like miniscule warts or bubbles.

Habitat and Season
Single, scattered or in clusters on decaying coniferous logs, stumps, snags and branches. Occasionally on decaying hardwood logs and stumps. August to November.

Found on very rotted pine or hemlock logs.

1–3" wide

1–2" tall

Flesh is rubbery.

Toothed Jelly

Note translucence.

Aug.–Nov.

Lemon Drops *Bisporella citrina*

This is one of the most commonly encountered cup fungi in New England for good reason. For one thing, its bright yellow color is an excellent public advertisement for it. For another, it fruits gregariously, so if you see one specimen, you'll usually see a great swarm of specimens. Likewise, you can find it year-round. Fruiting bodies are cup or saucer-shaped to irregularly round or flattened and bright lemon yellow. They rest stalkless or with a rudimentary stalk on their chosen substrate. The fruiting bodies of *Bisporella sulfurina*, a somewhat similar but less common species, are fused at the base.

Lemon Drops may look like actual lemon drops, but they're inedible.

Habitat and Season
In groups or extremely large clusters on decorticated or barkless wood. Year-round.

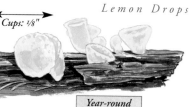

Lemon Drops

Cups: 1/8"

Year-round

Witch's Butter *Tremella mesenterica*

Although it parasitizes the mycelia of crust fungi, this cheery yellow or yellow-orange jelly is doubtless the creation of a good witch. It fruits in convoluted masses (*mesenterica* means "middle intestine") that become pallid or bloblike when waterlogged. The upright or arched lobes are responsible for spore production. Dried specimens are hard, but typically revive in wet weather. Young fruiting bodies sometimes look like cup fungi, but just wait—they'll become gelatinous and convoluted in a short while.

Butter Buddies
The very similar Orange Tree Brain (*Dacrymyces palmatus*) fruits on dead conifers, while Brown Witch's Butter (*Exidia recisa*) is cinnamon-brown and fruits on hardwoods, especially beech.

Habitat and Season
Single or in clusters on decaying hardwood twigs, limbs and branches. Year-round.

1–4" wide

Year-round

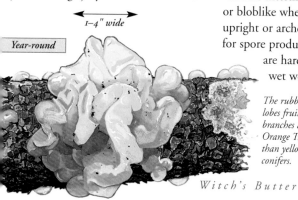

The rubbery orange mass of dense lobes fruits on dead hardwood branches and stumps. The similar Orange Tree Brain is more orange than yellow and fruits on dead conifers.

Witch's Butter

Asian Beauty *Radulomyces copelandii*

In December 2009, I found my first Asian Beauty on a big maple log in Topsfield, Massachusetts. It turned out that this was the first time the species had been seen anywhere in the Western Hemisphere. For Asian Beauties are, or were, an exclusively Asian species. Since that initial discovery, I've found Asian Beauties at quite a number of different sites in eastern Massachusetts.

The species is characterized by densely crowded, long (10 to 14 mm) spines that end in a sharp point. These spines are white to yellowish, becoming buff to brownish in age. Asian Beauties don't have a cap or stem. Instead they grow directly from their woody substrate. Specifically, they grow out of the cracks in that substrate's bark, possibly using those cracks for moisture as well as insulation. Fruiting bodies usually extend for as long as a crack itself extends.

The Asian Beauty fruits not only when other fleshy fungi fruit, but also during the winter. It probably has some

Teeth: ⅓–¾"

The teeth are among the longest of any tooth-bearing fungus.

as-yet undetermined chemical (a novel glycoprotein or form of trehalose?) that keeps it from freezing solid.

Heroine or Villainess?
An invasive fungus is not unlike an invasive plant: when it takes over a habitat, it nudges aside native species. Formerly resident only in Asia, this species is now showing up outside of Boston with some frequency. Is it nudging aside native species? Might it in fact be happily co-existing with native fungi? Or do either of these questions matter, since it's a wood decayer, and is thus performing an environmental service? At this point, the species might be called the Mysterious Asian Beauty, since we don't have the answers to any of these questions yet.

Habitat and Season
On hardwood logs, especially oak and maple. Year-round.

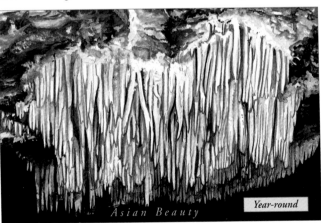

Typical growth habit is in the cracks and crevices of hardwood bark.

Asian Beauty

Year-round

Dog's Nose Fungus *Peridoxylon petersii (Camarops petersii)*

Not so long ago, the Dog's Nose Fungus was quite rare in New England. Nowadays it's still uncommon, but it's certainly not rare. Formerly a southern species, it may be moving north with climate change. Or perhaps the decline of logging has been a blessing to it—it grows almost exclusively on old oak logs, and since there are now more old oak trees, there are also more old oak logs.

Unlike an actual dog's nose, the species has a pink membranous veil when young and very large perithecia when mature. The fruiting body is jet-black, shiny, circular to cushion-shaped and sometimes has a narrow base. If you touch it, your fingers will be coated with black spores. Display these fingers proudly, as not many of your acquaintances will have experienced "Peridoxylon Finger." The species often smells like creosote.

Note perithecia all over the surface of the fruiting body.

Fungus: 1– 4½"

Grows only on old oak logs.

July – Oct.

Dog's Nose Fungus

Habitat and Season
On old oak logs. Formerly on American Chestnut logs. July to October.

No other fungus looks so much like a dog's nose!

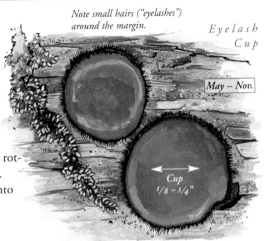

Note small hairs ("eyelashes") around the margin.

Eyelash Cup

May – Nov.

Cup 1/8 – 3/4"

Eyelash Cup *Scutellinia scutellata*

The eyelashes on this beguiling "asco" would make any fashion model green with envy. Of course, they're not really eyelashes, but stiff black hyphal hairs that may or may not help the fungus absorb moisture. The fruiting body is spherical to knoblike at first, but opens to reveal a bright red, scarlet or orange fertile surface. In addition to the margin, its exterior (underside) is often decorated with eyelash-like hairs. A similar species, *Scutellinia setosa*, is somewhat smaller, paler in color and even sometimes white.

Habitat and Season

In groups or dense clusters on rotten, often moss-covered wood. May to October, sometimes into November.

Green Stain *Chlorociboria aeruginascens (Chlorosplenium aeruginascens)*

The greenish or greenish-blue color you often see on logs is not spray paint or a fading trail blaze, but discoloration caused by the mycelium of this asco. The stain was once used for Tunbridge ware—decorative wooden objects inlaid with strips of colored veneer. One of the chemicals responsible for it, xylindein, is currently being investigated as a possible anti-carcinogen.

The mycelium also produces greenish or greenish-blue cup-shaped fruiting bodies, but they're encountered far less often than the stain. Maybe they're just overlooked, for a really hefty one might be ⅓ of an inch in diameter. The stalk is even more petite... seldom more than ¼ of an inch long.

Habitat and Season

Usually scattered along hardwood logs. July to late October, but the stain can be seen on decaying wood all year-round.

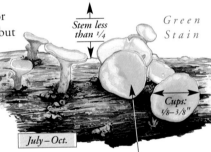

Green Stain

Stem less than ¼

Cups: 1/8 – 3/8"

July – Oct.

Fruiting bodies are tiny cup-shaped growths with stems less than 1/10-inch high.

The blue-green-stained wood is evident all year-round.

Common Brown Cup *Peziza varia*

Unless you count Gray Cup, which lies hidden under logs, *Peziza varia* is the cup fungus you're most likely to encounter in New England. Fruiting bodies are round when young, but assume a cup or saucer shape as they mature. In age, the fragile margin is usually wavy, recurved or broken. The inner surface is some shade of brown, while the outer surface tends to be lighter, occasionally with a few grayish tinges. The point of attachment is white. Several other brown *Pezizas* are so similar that they can't be distinguished in the field.

Numbers Game

You might see clouds of spores arising from this *Peziza* (or other cup fungi) when it's handled or when you blow on it. If ejected individually, these spores might travel only a few millimeters, but they synchronize their ejections to create a localized air stream, which allows them to travel a foot or more.

Cellar Dweller

Wet or rotting masonry provides a congenial substrate for this and several other *Pezizas*, which is why you might find them on your basement floor.

Habitat and Season

Single or in groups on rotting hardwood trunks and logs. Also in wet basements and on mulch and wood chips. May to November.

Brown Cup

Cups: ¾– 5"

May–Nov.

Cups often look tattered in age.

Gray Cup *Mollisia cinerea*

If you're suffering from mycological cabin fever in the winter, you can get a quick cure by lifting up a hardwood log. When you do, there's a good chance that you'll see a small gray cup fungus called *Mollisia cinerea*. With luck, you might find several hundred of these stalkless ascos under the same log. Each fruiting body will be more or less cup or saucer-shaped, but wavy or irregular in age. Often they're crowded together so closely that only the gray color will tell you what they are. Many specimens tend to be tinged yellow, with a dark margin. *Mollisia cinerea* is probably a species complex that includes a number of microscopically different gray cups.

Cups: ¼–¾"

Year-round

Gray Cup

Gray Cups are often squashed together.

Habitat and Season

Scattered or densely crowded under hardwood logs. Year-round.

Polypores

*A*lthough commonly called bracket fungi, only a relatively small percentage of polypores are actually bracket-shaped. Some are shaped like wedges of cheese, while many others are resupinate—their fruiting bodies lie flat against a substrate. Most resupinate polypores have neither cap nor stem, only pores.

Almost all polypores have pores which may be round, hexagonal or even mazelike. All but a few grow on living or dead wood. If there's an old stump in your vicinity, you'll probably find at least one polypore species growing on it. In the absence of a fruiting body, you can often tell if a polypore's mycelium has been at work on that stump by looking for outer signs of inner decay —cracks, swellings, carpenter ants, etc.

Most polypores are annuals, but some species can continue to grow as long as they're getting nutrients from their wood of choice. A perennial polypore is somehow a comforting sight. I once grew so fond of a 20+ year old Artist's Conk that I was heartbroken when it died.

Birch Polypore

Artist's Conk *Ganoderma applanatum*

*T*his is probably the best-known polypore or bracket fungus in North America. Mature specimens can be two or three feet wide and over 50 years old. Near Alexander Creek, Alaska, there's an Artist's Conk that's reputedly 1/4 mile wide and several thousand years old. Or so the local Dene informed me. I once saw a some-what smaller specimen in Maine being used as a bed by two raccoons, presumably mates.

Caps are fan-shaped or semi-circular, shelf-like to hoof-like, crusty, concentrically furrowed or at least zoned, tuberculate (warty) in age and gray, brown or gray-black. The white pore surface bruises brown, a fact that has made it a popular canvas for artists (see accompanying illustration). The species produces trillions of spores annually, so it's not unusual to find Artist's

Perennial, year-round

Conks literally blanketed by their own brown spores or the surrounding vegetation, formerly green, covered with brown spores, too.

Since an Artist's Conk's surface stains dark, you can draw intricate designs on it. Or you can leave notes on it.

Thanks for buying this book

Habitat and Season

Solitary or in overlapping clusters on decaying hardwoods. Year-round.

Artist's Conk

The number of spores released daily from a single fruiting body is enormous—in the billions.

Shelf: 2–12"

Varnish Shelf *Ganoderma lucidum*

This species looks like a semi-circular or kidney-shaped version of a Japanese lacquer box. Its seemingly varnished surface highlights its cap colors—concentric zones of dark red, reddish-brown, orange-brown and golden-brown, along with a white or yellowish margin. Certain specimens have much brighter colors, not to mention a more lacquered finish, than others. The pore surface is off-white to yellowish, becoming brown with age or if bruised. Some specimens have a reddish stalk no less lacquered than their caps. The Hemlock Varnish Shelf *(Ganoderma tsugae)* can be distinguished from *G. lucidum* by the fact that it grows on conifers, especially hemlock, while *G. lucidum* grows on hardwoods.

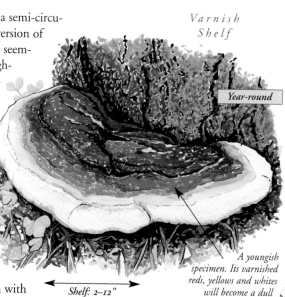

Varnish Shelf

Year-round

Shelf: 2–12"

A youngish specimen. Its varnished reds, yellows and whites will become a dull reddish-brown in age.

Habitat and Season

Single or clustered on living hardwoods: maples and oaks. May also grow on stumps and roots of some other broadleaf trees. Year-round.

Ling Chi

Forms of *G. lucidum* with a cap and stem are probably Ling Chi, a medicinal fungus described in Chinese texts more than 4000 years ago. Of the 365 species of wood, grasses, herbs, furs, animals and stones utilized by traditional Chinese medicine, Ling Chi was placed at the very top, and called "Herb of Spiritual Potency." In modern times, it's been used in Asia to treat cancer and respiratory diseases. Modern western science has recently begun to realize the potential of *G. lucidum* to stimulate the human immune system. Whether it also confers immortality on its users, as ancient Chinese sages claimed, remains to be seen.

Hemlock Varnish Shelf (Ganoderma tsugae) is similar but is only found on hemlocks and other conifers.

Hemlock Varnish Shelf

Red-belted Polypore
Fomitopsis pinicola

Despite its common name, the Red-belted Polypore is almost as likely to have a white or yellow belt (margin) as a red belt. Its scientific name suggests that it inhabits only pines, but you can frequently find it on hardwoods. In fact, it can be found on dozens of different tree species. Given such promiscuity, perhaps a better scientific name might be *Fomitopsis casanova*.

The fruiting body can be shelf-like, hoof-like or bracket-like. The cap usually has a varnished sheen and concentric zones of red, red-brown or brown that become mostly black near the point of attachment. The whitish pore surface slowly stains yellow when bruised, then becomes a dull brown in age. More common in the northern part of New England than the southern part.

Habitat and Season
Single or in groups on stumps and logs of conifers and hardwoods. Sometimes on living trees. Year-round.

Apparently not a picky fungus: F. pinicola has been recorded on more than 100 different species of tree hosts.

Shelf: 2–12"

Year-round

Red-belted Polypore

The glossy lacquer-like sheen coating this attractive species will actually melt when a match is held to it.

Birch Polypore
Piptoporus betulinus

Another species that grows only on birch stumps, logs and occasionally living trees. Its immature fruiting body has the look and feel of a rubber ball and, like a rubber ball, lacks pores. The white to grayish cap gradually becomes shelflike or kidney-shaped, acquiring pores along the way. These pores are white to gray-white and round, but in age split and become almost toothlike. The margin usually forms a curblike rim around the pore surface. The stem (when present) is short and stubby.

Multi-faceted Fungus
5,300-year old Tyrolean Ice Man Ötzi, discovered in 1991, had two polypores— the Birch Polypore and the Tinder Polypore (see page

Birch is its exclusive host.

Ötzi trudging to his high-altitude fate.

105)—among his possessions. He probably made a decoction of the former to rid himself of intestinal worms. Early New Englanders used the Birch Polypore as a razor strop; until recently, entomologists used it for mounting insect specimens; and the present-day Cree of northern Quebec (like Ötzi) make a medicinal tea from it. The Cree don't like the polypore's bitter flavor (due to a compound called Betulinic Acid), so they assume their alimentary parasites also won't like the flavor and will thus vacate the premises upon coming into contact with it.

Habitat and Season
Exclusively on birch, particularly Paper Birch and Yellow Birch. Year-round.

Year-round

Bracket: 2–10"

Almost looks inflatable!

The smooth cap and inrolled rim distinguish this fungus from similar polypores.

Birch Polypore

Cheese Polypore
Tyromyces chioneus

The wedgelike shape, spongy texture and often fragrant aroma of this species suggests that it's a refugee from the dairy section of a grocery store. The stalkless caps are smooth to finely hairy, pure white to watery white, becoming yellowish or pale gray in age. The pore surface is white to creamy-white or yellowish. The Blue Cheese Polypore (*Oligoporus caesius*) is similar, but has blue-gray tints on its cap and pore surface. Despite their names, neither of these species is edible.

June – Nov.

Cap: ³⁄₈ – 4"

Cheese Polypore

What is it? Since cheese doesn't usually grow on logs, it must be a cheese polypore!

Habitat and Season
Solitary, scattered or in groups on hardwood stumps and logs. June to November.

Milk-white Toothed Polypore *Irpex lacteus*

Year-round

←— Fungus: 1–12" —→

Milk-white Toothed Polypore

Chaga *Inonotus obliquus*

Chaga looks more like a wood burl gone awry than the fruiting body of a polypore. In fact, it isn't the fruiting body of a polypore at all, but a hardened mass of hyphae erupting through the bark of its birch tree host. This eruption has been variously referred to as a sclerotium, a false conk and a sterile conk. The actual fruiting body, which is small, grayish and resupinate, usually doesn't fruit until the host tree is dead.

The Milk-white Toothed Polypore lies flat against its substrate, but sometimes makes a perfunctory effort to form a series of caps, with the result that you often see what looks like half-completed caps projecting from its fruiting body (mycological term: effused-reflexed). But caps or no caps, it can spread for quite a distance on its substrate—I've seen Milk-white Toothed Polypores extend for ten feet or more along a dead branch. Very young specimens have pores, but older specimens have jagged-looking white teeth, which makes this species the very opposite of us humans: we start out with teeth, but end up with pores. The polypore's teeth (sometimes our teeth, too) become yellow, brownish and even bent in age.

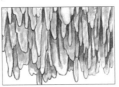

A dental nightmare — teeth are often very jagged-looking as well as yellow or even brown in age.

Habitat and Season

On dead deciduous wood. Very common on fallen branches. Year-round.

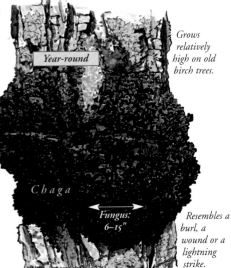

Year-round

Grows relatively high on old birch trees.

Chaga

←— Fungus: 6–15" —→

Resembles a burl, a wound or a lightning strike.

A Chaga's outer portion is blackish, deeply cracked, irregularly shaped and quite hard. The inner portion is bright yellow to rust brown, punky and often contains fragments of partially decayed bark. If you excavate the blackish exterior and find a blackish interior, then you're probably excavating a burl, not Chaga. Or perhaps burnt wood: the species is also called Clinker Polypore because looks like it's been burned and fused together.

Healthier than Vodka

The word *chaga* comes from Russia, where a decoction of the species' blackened mass has long been used as an anti-carcinogen and immune system potentiator. In New England, I often see Russians or people of Russian descent roaming birch groves in search of Chaga. Often they'll be carrying ropes and harnesses so they can climb up to the object of their quest. A Russian friend of mine eschews such burdensome equipment and simply shoots down Chagas with a shotgun.

Habitat and Season

On living and dead birch trees. Reported on maple. Year-round.

Rusty-gilled Polypore *Gloeophyllum separium*

Probably all polypores carry the gene for gills, but this species is one of the few that decided to do something about it, although it often seems to mix its gills with pores or even turn its gills into something akin to a labyrinth. The cap has yellow-red, rusty-red or brown concentric zones, along with a whitish margin. Older specimens tend to be more universally brownish. The gills are light golden brown or umber brown. Both young and old specimens have a matting of hairs on their caps. Another species, the Gilled Polypore (*Lenzites betulina*), has even more elongated gills as well as an even hairier cap.

A Real Rotter

This species causes brown rot damage in the structural wood of houses, fences, utility poles, bridges and railway ties. It has a special liking for wood treated with creosote!

Habitat and Season

Single or in groups on coniferous wood. June to October, but sometimes overwinters.

The typically schizophrenic underside of a Rusty-gilled Polypore.

Cap: 1-4"

Rusty-gilled Polypore

June – Oct.

Annual to Perennial; may overwinter.

Turkey Tail
Trametes versicolor

The ubiquitous Turkey Tail is probably 10 or 15 different species all lumped together under the name of a single avian body part. Even so, both the genus and species names are apt. *Trametes* means, "one who is thin," and *versicolor* means, "variously colored." The fruiting body is thin and leathery, forming rosettes on top of its chosen substrate and overlapping clusters

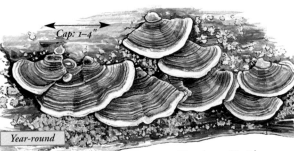

Always fruits in large groups in clusters, rosettes or tiers.

Cap: 1–4"

Year-round

Turkey Tail

on the side of that substrate. The fan-shaped cap's various colors include zones of gray, black, tan, orange, brown, green (due to algae) and yellow-buff, mix or match. The pore surface is whitish, but turns yellow, tan or gray in age. The pores are very small, but at least they're pores. An ostensibly similar species, the False Turkey Tail (*Stereum ostrea*), is a crust fungus and doesn't have any pores at all. Both species resemble the flared tail of a tom turkey.

Habitat and Season
In groups, clusters, rosettes and tiers on hardwood logs. Very common on stumps in areas where there's been logging. Year-round.

Rot On

The Turkey Tail's enzymes break down the lignin in dead wood, giving that wood the bleached look that's called white rot. Most polypores are white rotters. Brown rotters break down the cellulose in (primarily) conifers, with the result that the wood has a brown cubical design. While a white rotter can switch gears and engage in brown rot, a brown rotter cannot: it's stuck in the box or perhaps the cube.

Dryad's Saddle
Polyporus squamosus

The flattened, red-brown scales on the cap give this species its alternative name, Pheasant's Back Polypore. These scales are concentrically arranged on the dry, cream to yellowish-brown cap surface. The cap may be circular or

May – Nov.

Cap: 2–12"

Dryad's Saddle

Also called Pheasant's Back Polypore because of its similarity to the tail feathers of the non-native Ring-necked Pheasant.

fan-shaped and usually has a thin margin. It's often depressed or funnel-like. The flesh is soft in young specimens, but becomes corky and tough in age. The stubby lateral stem is tough in youth as well as age. Pores are relatively large, cream-colored and angular.

The Dryad's Saddle is a white rotter, but it performs its rotting duties at such a slow, even genteel pace that you wonder whether it would rather be doing something else... such as hosting dryads.

Habitat and Season

Single or in overlapping clusters on living and dead hardwoods. Common in urban areas. May to November.

Chicken of the Woods (Sulphur Shelf)

Laetiporus sulphureus

This typically large polypore starts out as a yellow, rubbery knob emerging from the host wood. But that's only a humble prelude to the development of multiple overlapping and clustered brackets with bright yellow-orange or salmon tops and intensely yellow undersides. Often, there are

The pale yellow inner flesh is firm but succulent, much softer near the margin and tougher near the point of attachment to the wood.

Note the radial furrowing.

enough colorful brackets to occupy the entire side of a living tree trunk or solidly blanket a sizable log.

The caps are flat, semi-circular or fan-shaped with a thick, rounded margin, which, in larger brackets, is usually lobed and wavy. The upper surface has suede-like soft matted hairs. The fertile underside of the bracket is bright sulphur-yellow with pores so small they are barely visible without magnification.

If you see a specimen with a white pore surface growing at the base of a tree or stump,

Shelf: 2–16"

May – Oct.

Chicken of the Woods

it should not be confused with a "dead chicken"—the white, crumbly remains of last year's yellow variety. Rather, it's a separate species *(Laetiporus cincinnatus).*

A Word of Caution

The Chicken of the Woods is an excellent edible, but it's been known to cause gastric upset in some individuals. Whether this is because of resident bacteria in its flesh or the presence of a toxin that produces an idiosyncratic reaction in certain diners has yet to be determined. Regardless of the cause, you should eat only a small portion of a well-cooked specimen the first time you try it, and if you're feeling fine the next day, it's likely that you won't need to go on a chicken-free diet.

Habitat and Season

Solitary, in overlapping clusters or forming rosettes on hardwood (especially oak) trunks, logs and stumps. May to October.

Hen of the Woods (Maitake)
Grifola frondosa

Several years ago, a friend of mine found a 58-pound Hen of the Woods just west of Boston. This was not an extremely overweight barnyard fowl, but a polypore whose numerous caps resemble the fluffed-up hind section of a hen. Maitake (see *A Universal Panacea,* below) is an increasingly popular common name for the same species.

A typical Hen of the Woods has compound clusters of fan-shaped or spoon-shaped caps growing laterally from a robust branched stem. Individual caps are gray to grayish-brown and possess wavy margins. The pores are white or cream-colored and angular. The usually rudimentary stem is tough and white to grayish. A similar species, the Black Staining Polypore *(Meripilus sumstinei),* has pores that bruise dark brown or black, along with fleshier caps. For culinary purposes,

Fruiting Body: 12–24"

Always grows at the base of a hardwood tree.

Numerous caps resemble the fluffed up rear of a hen— hence its common name.

Aug.–Oct.

Caps: 3/8–3"

Hen of the Woods

you can afford to make a mistake: both species are excellent edibles.

A Universal Panacea

Recent books on medicinal mushrooms have made great claims for Maitake. For example, it can control diabetes, lower cholesterol, help with bladder and prostrate cancer, protect the liver, treat edema and actively fight HIV. For me, the species' most valuable property is culinary—a sautéed Hen of the Woods actively fights bored taste buds.

Habitat and Season

Solitary or in clustered groups at the base of hardwoods, particularly maple and oak. Saprobic or weakly parasitic. August to October or early November.

Tinder Polypore (Hoof Fungus)
Fomes fomentarius

The older it gets, the more hoof-shaped a *Fomes fomentarius* fruiting body becomes, until it ends up looking like the hoof of a horse glued to the side of a tree. Many older specimens are much taller than they are wide, which makes them look like a horse's hoof with Marfan's Syndrome. The cap of this hard as well as hardy perennial has concentric zones with different shades of gray set apart by grooves and rounded, wavy ridges. The pore surface is brown, with very small round pores. *F. fomentarius* is a heart rot fungus. This means that it can't

Up to 10"

2–6"

Year-round

Note concentric rings on fruiting body.

Tinder Polypore

digest healthy wood, so it digests only the non-living tissue of a tree's heartwood.

The Ice Man Carryeth

As its common name suggests, the Tinder Polypore can be used as a firestarter. A spark from rubbed flints is often enough to ignite its exposed tubes if they're dry. Since the Tyrolean Ice Man Ötzi carried chunks of the polypore in his pouch, he might have been using it in this time-honored fashion. But he might also have been using it for the antibacterial properties that it shares with a number of other polypores. Or he might even have been using it as a smudge against evil spirits. Or prior to venturing onto the glacier that proved to be his final home, he could have been using it as an insect smudge: a smoldering specimen does a good job keeping mosquitoes and other biting insects at bay.

Habitat and Season

Single to many on decaying hardwoods, especially birch and beech. Year-round.

Big Berk

Bondarzewia berkeleyi

Whenever I see a large Big Berk, I do a double take, because its size (up to 3 feet in diameter) suggests an age of giants. Maybe a *T. rex* will come crashing out of the woods while I'm gazing at one of these humungous polypores?

Big Berk is an annual polypore whose spongy-tough caps develop from a gnarly root base. The individual caps can be white, gray or yellowish tan. The pores are no less variable—they can be circular, angular or even labyrinthine. DNA data has recently placed Big Berk in the same group as *Russulas*. A giant polypore that's a first cousin to a gilled mushroom? Anyone who's looked at both under a microscope won't be surprised by this, since their spores have a similar ornamentation around the edges.

The largest of all New England polypores. For scale purposes, here's a typical Big Berk alongside this book's not necessarily diminutive author.

Why Bondarzewia?

The genus was named for the Russian mycologist Apollinaris Semenovich Bondartsev, a man so devoted to wood decay fungi that he was still scampering over roofs and climbing trees to study these fungi when he was well past the age of eighty. Not limited to large wood decayers, Bondartsev also wrote the first description of the Blue-gray Crust (*Byssocorticium alkovirens*).

Habitat and Season

In rosettes at the base of both living and dead hardwoods, especially oak and maple. June to October.

Each pileus (cap): 3–10"

Fruiting Body: 12–42" wide!

June– Oct.

Big Berk

Violet-toothed Polypore
Trichaptum biforme

When this species is fresh, the bright lavender color of its pore surface and cap margin will identify it for you. When it's dry, there are still several distinctive features: a hairy, zoned cap; angular pores that become jagged or toothlike in age; an extremely gregarious fruiting habit (you never find a solitary Violet-toothed Polypore); and the frequent presence of a tiny parasitic asco on its cap (see *Peewee Parasite*, below). It grows exclusively on hardwoods, while an almost identical species, *Trichaptum* *abietinum*, grows only on conifers. Both species are very common.

Peewee Parasite

Look for colonies of Black Matchsticks (*Phaeocalicium polyporaeum*) near the margin of the Violet-toothed Polypore.

Black Matchsticks
(Phaeocalicium polyporaeum)

Look hard, for this club-shaped asco is small...VERY small. The head is approximately $^1/_{32}$ of an inch wide, and the stem is $^1/_{16}$ of an inch long. The species looks like a matchstick shrunk down almost to the point of invisibility. Formerly called Stubble Lichen based on the erroneous assumption that it was a lichen.

Habitat and Season

In very large clusters on hardwood stumps, logs and decaying limbs. May to November, but old fruiting bodies can be found year-round.

Caps: 1/3 – 3"

Old fruiting bodies may be seen year-round.

Look for toothlike projections under the cap.

May – Nov.

Violet-toothed Polypore

Cinnabar-red Polypore
Pycnoporus cinnabarinus

As it is with people, so it is with fungi —beauty often lies hidden. This polypore's cap may be somewhat ordinary, but its bright red pore surface is quite lovely. It retains its color for quite a long time. Five years ago, I gave a

Typically features an orange cap and bright red pore surface.

Cap: 1–4"

Year-round

Cinnabar-red Polypore

woman friend a *Pycnoporus cinnabarinus* necklace, and its color still has not faded.

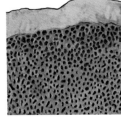

Pycnoporus pores

Caps are kidney-shaped, orange to dull reddish-orange, azonate and covered with warts and wrinkles in age. The pore surface, in the words of mycologist Gary Lincoff, "looks as if it had been seared by a hot iron." The pores themselves are usually more angular than round. With climate change, a similar, albeit much thinner southern species, *Pycnoporus sanguineus*, may start showing up in New England in the not too distant future.

Habitat and Season
Single or in groups on hardwood logs, especially cherry. Year-round.

Wasp's Nest Polypore
Coltriciella dependens

This species is considered rare, yet I've found it many times in the last few years. Either it's no longer rare, or nobody's looking in the right place. For most polypores grow on logs or beneath them, but very few tend to grow INSIDE them, as this one often does.

Coltriciella dependens looks exactly like a miniature wasp's nest, albeit an upside down one. In fact, it's the only polypore with a pendant fruiting body. The cap is white and very hairy when young,

Pores are variable in size and shape.

but becomes less hairy as well as rusty brown to a rich coffee brown in age. The large pores are angular or irregular, and the stalk is usually short, light brown and hairy. Stalkless specimens occasionally occur when the mycelium creates a fruiting body in a space too pinched or narrow to accommodate a stem.

Habitat and Season
Solitary or in fused groups either inside or under rotten logs. Year-round.

How cool is this? A polypore that looks almost exactly like an upside down wasp's nest!

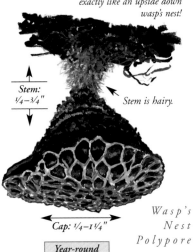

Stem: ¼–¾"

Stem is hairy.

Cap: ¼–1¼"

Year-round

Wasp's Nest Polypore

Thick Maze & Thin Maze Polypores
Daedalea quercina & Daedaleopsis confragosa

Like the Cinnabar-red Polypore, the caps of both these polypores are unexceptional—tough or corky, gray to brown and usually zoned or concentrically furrowed. But if you look beneath them, you won't see typical pores, not at all, but a gill-like labyrinth of pores. The Thick Maze Polypore's pores are much wider than those of the Thin Maze Polypore. Its pores are white and don't stain, while the latter's pores are white to brownish, more variable in shape and usually stain red or

Stains reddish or brown if bruised or handled.

Cap: 2–6"

Thin Maze Polypore

The narrow maze of this polypore would not accommodate even a skinny Minotaur.

brownish. Both genera derive their names from the mythical Greek Daedalus, best known for creating a labyrinth in which to house the bull-headed Minotaur.

Habitat and Season
The Thick Maze Polypore grows only on dead oak, but the Thin Maze Polypore can grow on virtually any type of dead or dying hardwood. Both species can be found year-round.

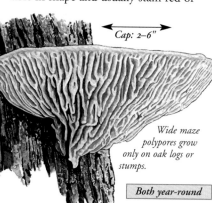

Cap: 2–6"

Wide maze polypores grow only on oak logs or stumps.

Both year-round

Thick Maze Polypore

Carbon Antlers
Xylaria hypoxylon

The so-called antlers on this species are its spore-bearing appendages. Like the "fingers" on its fellow Xylarian, Dead Man's Fingers, they're covered with the whitish powder of asexual spores (conidia) when they're immature. Sexually mature fruiting bodies are black and covered with ascus-bearing perithecia. Antlers range from one to six "points" and are far too small to mount on your mantelpiece. The stalk is usually ribbon-like to oval, tough and slightly hairy. Also called Candlesnuff Fungus.

Habitat and Season
Scattered or in clusters on dead or decaying wood. June to November, but sometimes overwinters.

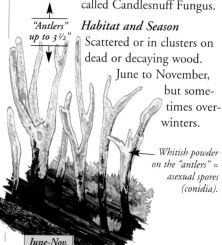

"Antlers" up to 3½"

Whitish powder on the "antlers" = asexual spores (conidia).

June-Nov.

Comb Tooth
Hericium americanum

This remarkable species resembles a giant mass of icicles that have appeared at a time of year when there shouldn't be any icicles. Numerous coral-like branches, each of which ends in clusters of teeth or spines, droop down from a robust, but seldom-visible support stem. The entire fruiting body is white, but becomes yellowish or brown in age. The Comb Tooth's consistency becomes increasingly tough in age, too. Also known as Waterfall Fungus, White Beard, Bearded Hedgehog, Big Tooth and (in France) *Pom Pom*.

July – Oct.

← 6–12" wide →

Fungus 8–20"

Habitat and Season
Single or in groups on the sides of decaying hardwood logs and stumps. July to October.

Has an uncanny resemblance to a bunch of icicles growing on a tree.

Comb Tooth

Crown-tipped Coral
Artomyces (Clavicorona) pyxidata

One of the few corals to grow on wood. Its fruiting body has multiple branches rising from a short, felty sterile base. The branches are attractively arranged in tiers with upper branches springing from the enlarged tips of lower branches (a candelabra-like effect). Branch tips are arranged in what seems to be a tiny crown. The body of the coral is pale yellow when young, but becomes yellowish, pinkish or tan in age.

Habitat and Season
Single or in small groups on dead hardwoods, especially willow and aspen. Late May to October.

Clusters: 2–5"

Crown-tipped Coral

May-Oct.

Name Game

The names of three Hericiums (H. americanum, H. coralloides *and* H. ramosum) *have been shifted about by taxonomists so often that it's surprising the species in question haven't gotten terminal motion sickness. In situations like this, all the amateur forager can do is try to identify his specimen based on the different names for the same species in different guidebooks... and chuckle. After all, it's only a game—a name game.*

Beech Balls *Hypoxylon fragiforme*

In New England, almost every dead or dying beech branch seems to have a complement of Beech Balls on it. Sometimes they're separated from each other; more often, they're fused together to form a crustlike mass. They're pink when young, brick red when mature and black when they're past their prime —i.e., no longer producing spores. The pimple-like perithecia on mature fruiting bodies tell you that you're looking at an asco. Many *Hypoxylons*, including this species, can live for several years, assuming they have enough wood to munch on.

Habitat and Season
On dead or soon-to-be-dead branches of beech trees. Year-round.

Beech Balls

"Balls": 1/8– 3/4"

Having dinner "on the beech"— they can live as long as they're able to get nutrients from their woody substrate—often four or five years.

Beech Balls are often fused together to form a crustlike mass.

Year-round

Crowded Parchment *Stereum rameale (complicatum)*

One of the most common fungi as well as one of the most crowded fungi in New England.

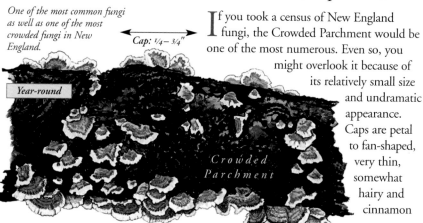

Cap: 1/4– 3/4"

Year-round

Crowded Parchment

If you took a census of New England fungi, the Crowded Parchment would be one of the most numerous. Even so, you might overlook it because of its relatively small size and undramatic appearance. Caps are petal to fan-shaped, very thin, somewhat hairy and cinnamon to reddish-brown with reddish zones and furrows. The fertile surface (underside) is smooth and fades from orange to a dull cream or cinnamon color. As befits its name, the Crowded Parchment consists of crowds, not individuals. It's not unusual to see several hundred gregarious fruiting bodies laterally fused or in dense clusters on a single branch.

Habitat and Season
In large numbers on dead hardwood branches and stumps. Year-round.

Blue-gray Crust *Byssocorticium atrovirens*

You might first mistake a crust fungus for a polypore, except that it doesn't have pores: it produces its spores on a smooth or warty resupinate fertile surface. In the case of the Blue-gray Crust, that fertile surface has a cottony, membranous texture that suggests a very dense cobweb. Along its growing edges is a mass of diffuse hyphae called cordons. You can easily pull these cordons or even bits of the main fruiting body off a log. The blue-gray color is so uncommon in crust fungi that you can almost identify the species by color alone. However, you might actually be identifying *Byssocorticium pulchrum*, a species so similar to this one that you can distinguish them only by spore size.

Habitat and Season
On both hardwood and softwood logs, especially oak. Probably mycorrhizal rather than saprobic. Year-round.

Blue-gray Crust

Fungus: ½–4"

Year-round

A crust fungus isn't always crusty. This one has a soft and cottony texture.

The fungal equivalent of a bathroom floor.

Ceramic Crust

Grows ONLY on oak logs.

"Tiles": ⅛–⅔"

Fruiting Body: up to 6" across

Year-round

Ceramic Crust *Xylobolus frustulatus*

Ceramic Crust resembles tile fragments that someone has done a lousy job of putting back together again. Its resupinate fruiting body is dirty white, pinkish, tan, gray or sometimes orange in color. The smooth or sometimes pimpled "tiles" are densely crowded, more or less polygonal and seemingly cracked. The species causes a white pocket rot (any rot localized in small areas) on oak logs, its almost exclusive substrate. I was once asked if the Ceramic Crust is edible. That's like asking if a bathroom floor is edible.

Unusual Fact
One of the antibacterial chemicals created by the Ceramic Crust is almost exactly the same as a chemical found in the wings of the male Northern Blue butterfly (*Lycaeides idas*), where it probably acts as a sex pheromone.

Habitat and Season
On or under oak logs. Year-round.

Black Knot *Apiosporina morbosa*

This fungus is fascinating in so far as a murderer can be fascinating, for it is a highly destructive pathogen of cherry trees. It starts out as an olive-brown swelling on a cherry branch and soon enlarges, ruptures and becomes blackened. During its two-year life cycle, it elongates along the branch and encircles it. The fungal growth interferes with the transmission of water and minerals and inhibits transfer of food produced by the leaves to other parts of the tree. The infected branches die and the tree is greatly weakened. In the second year, a "shuck split" opens up on the species' crustlike surface and releases spores. Also called "Shit on a Stick" in certain parts of New England.

Here's the Good News

Even as it's disposing of its host, the Black Knot is providing a home for various small insects as well as food for birds and other species of fungi. Turnabout is fair play.

Habitat and Season

On cherries, plum trees and other members of the genus *Prunus*. Year-round.

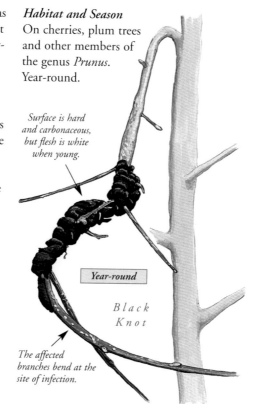

Surface is hard and carbonaceous, but flesh is white when young.

Year-round

Black Knot

The affected branches bend at the site of infection.

NON-GILLED *on* OTHER

I n this catch-all category, the species are not only parasitic, but most of them would also seem to be emulating Hollywood mad scientists in the way they transform the "Other:" the *Hypomyces* turns a *Russula* or *Lactarius* into an entirely different species called a Lobster; an *Entoloma* causes a Honey Mushroom to lose its characteristic cap-and-stem shape; *Rhizopus stolonifer* turns a bowl of strawberries into an inedible, gooey mess; and a *Cordyceps* eats away at its truffle host until that host completely falls to pieces. You would think a movie producer would approach one or more of these species with a contract, wouldn't you? Well, it hasn't happened yet...

The Pinecone Fungus is much nicer than any of these other species. Yes, it's still a parasite, but it doesn't have any interest in altering the shape of its host. What's more, it's cute enough to raise your blood sugar to near-toxic levels. As far as I know, no film producer has contacted it, either.

Lobster Mushroom *Hypomyces lactifluorum*

U nbeknownst to most people, there are lobsters in the New England woods. But these lobsters aren't crustaceans. Rather, they're a species of *Russula* or *Lactarius* parasitized by a *Hypomyces*, which, having no overt shape of its own, assumes the shape of its host. The orange to orange-red *Hypomyces* engulfs that host's cap, gills and stem in such a way that they appear to be out-of-focus to the casual viewer. Since the agent of this takeover is an asco, you'll see tiny pustule-like perithecia on its surface. It's usually impossible to determine the exact identity of the host, but presumably the *Hypomyces* knows. Not for it

a tiny moss-dwelling *Lactarius* or a small, seemingly inconsequential *Russula*: it seeks out the large and fleshy species, which is like choosing to dine on a big juicy steak rather than chicken liver.

Habitat and Season
On species of *Russula* and *Lactarius*, usually after wet weather. August to late October.

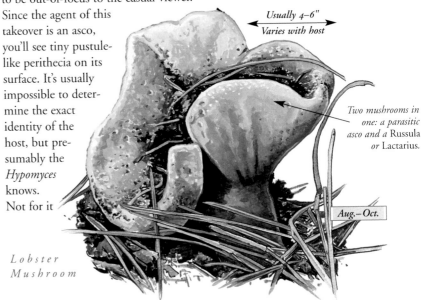

Usually 4–6"
Varies with host

Two mushrooms in one: a parasitic asco and a Russula *or* Lactarius.

Aug.– Oct.

Lobster Mushroom

Pinecone Fungus *Auriscalpium vulgare*

An almost foolproof mushroom to identify. It has a brown densely hairy cap, a brown densely hairy stem, and—here's what makes the ID a no-brainer—tiny teeth projecting from the underside of the cap. These teeth are whitish at first, but they soon become brown, too.

As the name suggests, the Pinecone Fungus grows exclusively on pinecones, albeit pinecones fallen to the ground.

Usually, it grows out of the side of the fallen cone. This makes it look like, in the words of mycologist Michael Kuo, "a little periscope sent up from a pinecone submarine."

Habitat and Season

Single or in small groups on several different types of pinecones. Occasionally on corncobs. August to late October.

Cap:
3/8–1 1/2"

If you look under the cap, you'll see a plethora of tiny teeth.

Pinecone Fungus

Stem:
1–3"

Usually grows out of the side of a pinecone.

Aug.–Oct.

Acorn Cup *Hymenoscyphus fructigenus*

Once you find this charming little asco, you'll never look at acorns in the same way again. In fact, you might find yourself looking for a *H. fructigenus* fruiting body on every acorn you see, which could turn a leisurely walk in the woods into a virtual stall. But don't look on fresh acorns: the species typically grows only on acorns left over from the previous year. The fruiting body consists of a white, cream-colored or yellow cup mounted on a similarly colored, usually very short stem.

You sometimes see these fruiting bodies in such dense clusters that they totally obscure the acorn.

Habitat and Season

Single or in clusters on acorns. Occasionally on hickory or beech nuts. July to October.

Acorn Cup

Cap up to 1/5"

Stem:
1/5"

Primarily found on last year's acorns.

July.–Oct.

Truffle Lover *Elaphocordyceps longisegimentis (Cordyceps canadensis)*

Cap:
¼ – ¾"

Stem:
1-6" tall

Dig very, very carefully, and you might find the object of its love—an Elaphomyces truffle.

Truffle Lover

Aug.–Nov.

While some *Cordyceps* parasitize insects, the Truffle Lover parasitizes a subterranean fungus—a warty, reddish-brown false truffle *(Elaphomyces granulatus)* that may or may not be mycorrhizal with conifers. It's not a good idea for you to eat this truffle unless you happen to be a *Cordyceps* yourself. For one thing, it's resolutely inedible; for another, *Elaphomyces* species absorb radioactive pollution with a high degree of efficiency.

The upper part or head of the *Cordyceps* is dark reddish to olive-black, irregularly rounded and dotted with ascus-bearing perithecia. Two-headed specimens are not unknown. The firm, frequently ridged or furrowed stem is yellow, becoming brownish yellow and usually bent in age. *C. capitata* is nearly identical, but has smaller spores. Unlike *C. sinensis* (see *Summer Plant, Winter Worm* sidebar), neither species has ever been associated with enhanced male sexual potency.

Habitat and Season
Single or scattered on *Elaphomyces* truffles in coniferous woods. August to November.

Summer Plant, Winter Worm

On the erroneous assumption that it's a single organism rather than a parasitic fungus and the caterpillar of a moth (Thitarodes sp.), the Chinese call Cordyceps sinensis "Summer Plant, Winter Worm." The species made headlines in 1993 when Chinese women runners broke nine different records in the Chinese National Games. It turned out that the ingestion of C. sinensis had been an important part of their training regimen.

According to the Chinese, the species doesn't simply boost a person's athletic prowess. It's also effective in the treatment of pulmonary problems and asthma; increases blood flow to the brain; fortifies the liver; and revives the male sexual organ from certain death. As a result of these attributes, almost every market in China will display huge piles of C. sinensis still attached to its host. Many of the specimens are brought from Tibet, where it seems only a matter of time before the species (and its host) are wiped out.

We live in a zoocentric world: we express concern, even outrage at the prospect of an animal becoming extinct, but the potential disappearance of a fungus leaves us unmoved. In most ecosystems, however, all species great and small play a necessary, often equally important role.

Aborted Honey (Aborted Entoloma) *Entoloma abortivum*

The aborted form of this species looks like a mass of amorphous tissue masquerading as a mushroom. That form is white to dove gray and lumpy, with small hairs hugging its surface. The abortifier (not the abortee!) is an *Entoloma* that possesses a convex, pale gray to grayish-brown cap with an inrolled or wavy margin. Its gills are decurrent, crowded and initially grayish, but soon become pink. The stem is colored like the cap, slightly hairy and often enlarged at the base. Aborted Entoloma is not a particularly good name; a more appropriate one would be Aborted Honey. So I'm happy to set a precedent by calling it that in this book.

The species is edible when fresh, but inedible if it shows any bacterial decay.

Just Desserts
In one corner, a lightweight *Entoloma*, and in the other corner, a heavyweight parasite called a Honey Mushroom— on which would you place your bet? In the old days, mycologists assumed the Honey Mushroom was the winner and gave it a technical knockout. More recently, it's been determined that the underdog *Entoloma* is actually the victor, or rather its mycelium is the victor, and that the Honey Mushroom was the one that got knocked out — i.e., aborted. A possible title for this match might be: *The Parasitizer Parasitized.*

Habitat and Season
Scattered or in groups on some sort of woody debris. Usually in mixed forests. August to October.

Aborted Entoloma

Aborted form:
1–4"

1–2"

A Honey Mushroom's #1 Enemy.

Aug.–Oct.

Horn Stalkball
Onygena equina

While most fungal species are very specific about their habitats, this odd little asco is almost insanely specific about its particular habitat: it grows only on the shed antlers, horns, and hooves of deer, sheep, and moose, dining on keratin or collagen. A powdery brown spore mass resides in its cap, which breaks open at maturity, and off go the spores.

Cap:
⅛ – ¼"

Stem:
¼ – ½"

The cap is warty and cream-colored, becoming reddish-brown. The cylindrical stem is smooth and whitish to brown. A similar species, *Onygena corvina*, grows on bird-feathers as well as owl pellets. Both species have a somewhat unpleasant odor.

Habitat & Season
On the rotting antlers, horns, and hooves of animals, especially ones so rotten that they're rather cheesy. Year-round.

One of the few fungi that eats keratin.

Year-round

Fuzzy Mold
Rhizopus stolonifer

I've cheated here and included a mold that commonly grows on bread, fruit, tomatoes and sweet potatoes. When it's mature, *Rhizopus stolonifer* looks less like a fungus than like some sort of small furry critter asleep on your strawberries. Each furry unit consists of a stem and a minute caplike sporangium laden with spores. At the base of the stem are rhizoids that resemble the roots of a plant rather than something you'd find with a fungus. *Rhizopus* ("root-foot") derives its name from these rhizoids.

Almost invisible caplike sporangia at the end of each "hair" house the spores.

Molds are seldom included in mushroom guidebooks, so why did I include one in this book? Because you're probably more likely to encounter *R. stolonifer* than any of the other species I've described, and also because (its potentially destructive disposition notwithstanding) it's altogether fascinating...

Habitat and Season
On fruit, bread, vegetables and sometimes us (it causes a rare infection called zygomycosis). Year-round.

A WINTER FORAY

It was late January, the temperature was just above freezing, and the weatherperson had predicted a snowstorm for eastern New England. Even so, I felt the urge to go out and look for mushrooms. When such urges come over me, I have no choice, none whatsoever, but to submit. So I donned the appropriate winter garb and took to the woods near Walden Pond in eastern Massachusetts.

At first I didn't find much, but as my eyes became accustomed to the perpetually failing light of winter, I started to see—mushrooms! On a hardwood log was a panoply of Split Gills, their delicate pinkish gills resembling miniature Japanese fans. I saw what seemed to be a fresh fruiting of Brown Witch's Butter (Exidia recisa) on a fallen beech branch. I also saw the Asian Beauty (Radulomyces copelandii) growing all along the cracks and crevices of an old oak log.

One discovery led to another. I found a bouquet of Orange Mock Oysters that boasted the species' characteristic (and characteristically foul) methane odor. Beneath a maple log, I observed perhaps a hundred delicate Gray Cups huddled together or spread out like daubs of gray paint on a canvas. Several fruitings of the Night Light made me wish that I could be here at night so that I could see their gills glow.

By the end of the afternoon, I had encountered twenty-five or thirty more species,

including Turkey Tails, Crowded Parchment, Thick and Thin Maze Polypores, Yellow Witch's Butter, Artist's Conks, Cheese Polypores, Birch Polypores, Lemon Drops, Purple Toothed Polypores, Milk White Toothed Polypores, Crimped Gills (Plicaturopsis crispa), several puffballs, Winter Polypores (Polyporus brumalis), a tiny Mycena (Mycena corticola) under a tree's bark, Ceramic Parchment, the Ochre Spreading Tooth (Steccherinum ochraceum), Tinder Polypores and a few white Crust Fungi.

Thus I went home with that feeling of satisfaction that comes after a successful foray. (P.S. It did in fact snow that evening.)

Night Light

Asian Beauty

Orange Mock Oyster

Gray Cups

Turkey Tails

Crowded Parchment

Thin Maze Polypore

Yellow Witch's Butter

Artist's Conks

Lemon Drops

Crimped Gills

Tinder Polypores

SLIME MOLDS

Slime molds are not molds, nor are they even fungi. By all rights, they should be included in books on protozoa, to which they're related, rather than books dealing with fungi. But the field characteristics of certain slime molds are so similar to fungi that even professional mycologists have been known to confuse the two. Likewise, they inhabit many of the same substrates that fungi inhabit.

Like fungi, slime molds reproduce via spores, but unlike fungi, their spores hatch tiny organisms that resemble amoebas. These organisms move, yes, move along a substrate in search of edible bacteria (they can spit out inedible bacteria). One particularly brisk species has been clocked at the speed of an inch per hour—not quite enough to win a marathon, but still. At a certain point, these moving entities clump together to form a large blob called a plasmodium. Later that blob shape-shifts into an often mushroom-like shape called a sporangium. It's in this latter phase that they create and disperse their spores. These two phases are so different that mycologist Gary Lincoff calls slime molds "the Dr. Jekylls and Mr. Hydes of the plant world."

Blackberry Slime
Metatrichia vesparum

The lidded fruiting bodies of this slime mold are wine-colored to dark reddish-black and joined together by a thick supporting stem. The lids themselves are more or less dome-shaped. Eventually, they break open, and you'll see something absolutely essential to the

The clusters arise from a single stalk.

survival of the species—a purplish-red mass that combines the Blackberry Slime's capillitium (threadlike filaments that support the spore mass) with its spores. As with most slime molds, the capillitium expedites the release of spores. Also known as Many Headed Slime, Wasp Nest Slime and Multi-Goblet Slime.

Habitat and Season
On well-rotted wood. July to October.

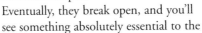

The blue-black lustered fruitbodies (sporangia) look a lot like blackberries.

Blackberry Slime

July – Oct.

Chocolate Tube Slime
Stemonitis species

Hard to identify as to species, but easy to identify as to genus, the Chocolate Tube Slime consists of dozens of erect, brown tubes mounted on thin, seemingly polished black stems. If these tubes are mature, you can blow on them, and a thick cloud of violet-brown spores will burst into the air. The tubes are the sporangial phase of a *Stemonitis*. If you see dozens of shiny white translucent balls that appear to be tightly glued together in the vicinity of these tubes, you've merely found the immature form, not a different species. You can often find enormous fruitings of the Chocolate Tube Slime on a single log. Also known as the Pipecleaner Slime.

Habitat and Season
On decaying wood, logs and sometimes leaves. May to October.

Like most slime molds, the Chocolate Tube Slime grows on decaying wood.

Stem: ¼–1"

The cylindrical brown structures are the sporangia.

Different species of Stemonitis can only be identified by microscopic features.

May-Oct.

Chocolate Tube Slime

Wolf's Milk Slime
Lycogala epidendrum

Fruiting Body: ⅛ – ⅝"

Filled with grayish spore powder when mature.

Also called Toothpaste Slime because of the pink goo inside young specimens.

Year-round

Wolf's Milk Slime

Although this species seems to resemble a miniature puffball, it's actually a very common slime mold. The round fruiting bodies are pinkish when young, but gray to lead-colored when mature. The salmon-pink paste inside young specimens gives the species its common name. For Wolf's Milk is a spurge (*Euphorbia esula*) that leaks an acrid, milky juice. In mature *L. epidendrum* specimens, the paste loses its gooey consistency and becomes a grayish to yellowish spore mass. As with the previous species (not to mention puffballs), it's highly rewarding to blow on or poke a mature *L. epidendrum* and watch the spores explode into the air. A similar species, *Lycogala flavofuscum*, has considerably larger as well as more brittle fruiting bodies.

Habitat and Season
Scattered or clustered on dead wood. Year-round.

Scrambled Egg Slime
Fuligo septica

The most egalitarian of slime molds, this species can be round, cushion-shaped or bloblike, not to mention yellow, bright pink, red, whitish, tan or lilac-colored. Likewise, it can grow in leaf litter and wood mulch as well as on plants and logs. And while it can indeed look like scrambled eggs, it can also look like, well, mycologist Sam Ristich once described a large specimen as "resembling the vomit of six Great Danes."

Although *Fuligo septica* seems to disturb homeowners when they find it in their mulched gardens or on their lawns, it's completely harmless. In fact, it's a prized edible in certain parts of Mexico, where it's known as *Caca da Luna* (Shit of the Moon). A pity this highly poetic name has not caught on north of the border...

Habitat and Season
On logs, wood mulch, plants, grass, etc. May to October.

The largest of all slime molds—one particularly large specimen was compared by mycologist Sam Ristich to "the vomit of 6 Great Danes."

Fruiting Body: 1–12"

Scrambled Egg Slime

May–Oct.

TITLES OF INTEREST

Arora, D. 1986. *Mushrooms Demystified*. Berkley, CA: Ten Speed Press.

Barron, G. 1999. *Mushrooms of Northeast North America*. Edmonton, AB: Lone Pine Press.

Bessette, A. 1995. *Mushrooms of North America in Color*. Syracuse, NY: Syracuse University.

Bessette, A.R., A. Bessette, and W. Neill. 2001. *Mushrooms of Cape Cod and the National Seashore*. Syracuse, NY: Syracuse University

Bessette, A., A. R. Bessette and D. W. Fischer. 1997. *Mushrooms of Northeastern North America*. Syracuse, NY: Syracuse University.

Binyon, D. et al. 2008. *Macrofungi Associated with Oaks of Eastern North America*. Morgantown, WV: West Virginia University Press.

Glick, P. G. 1979. *The Mushroom Trailguide*. New York, NY: Holt, Rinehart and Winston.

Hudler, G. W. 1998. *Magical Mushrooms, Mischievous Molds*. Princeton, NJ: Princeton University Press.

Kauffman, C.H. 1971. *Gilled Mushrooms of Michigan and the Great Lakes Region, 2 vols*. New York, NY: Dover Publications.

Kendrick, B. 1992. *The Fifth Kingdom*. Waterloo, Ontario: University of Waterloo.

Kuo, M. 2010. *100 Cool Mushrooms*. Ann Arbor: University of Michigan Press.

Laessoe, T., and G. Lincoff. 2002. *Smithsonian Handbooks: Mushrooms*. New York, NY: DK Publishing.

Lincoff, G. 1984. *The Audubon Society Field Guide to North American Mushrooms*. New York, NY: Knopf.

McKnight, K. H., and V. B. McKnight. 1987. *A Field Guide to Mushrooms of North American*. New York, NY: Houghton Mifflin.

McIlvaine, C., and R. K. Macadam. 1973. *One Thousand American Fungi*. New York, NY: Dover Publications.

Miller Jr., O. K., and H. H. Miller. 2006. *North American Mushrooms*. Gilford, CT: Falcon Guide.

Moore, D. 2001. *Slayers, Saviors, Servants, and Sex: An Expose of Kingdom Fungi*. Manchester, England: Springer

Phillips, R. 2005. *Mushrooms and other Fungi of North America*. Buffalo, NY: Firefly Books.

Schaechter, E. 1998. *In the Company of Mushrooms*. Cambridge, MA: Harvard University Press.

Smith, H. V., and A. H. Smith. 1981. *How to Know the Non-Gilled Fleshy Fungi*. Dubuque, IA: Wm. C. Brown.

Smith, A. H., H. V. Smith and N. Weber. 1979. *How to Know the Gilled Mushrooms*. Dubuque, IA: Wm. C. Brown.

Stephenson, S. 2010. *The Kingdom Fungi*. Portland, OR: Timber Press

GLOSSARY

adnate: gills attached to the stalk without a notch

adnexed: gills attached to the stalk with a notch

annular zone: a ring on the stalk derived from the partial veil

annulus: a ring on the stalk

apex: the uppermost portion of the stalk

ascomycetes: a major group of fungi that includes species that produce spores in asci (sacs)

ascospore: spore formed within an ascus (sac)

ascus: a sac-like structure where the ascospores are formed (*asci*: plural)

attached: gills joined to the stalk

basal: located at the base of a structure such as a stalk

basidiospore: a spore formed on a basidium

basidium: a club-shaped structure on which the spores are formed (*basidia*: plural)

basidiomycetes: a major group of fungi that includes gilled mushrooms

bracket: shelflike fruiting body produced by wood-rotting basidiomycetes

bruising: changing color when handled

button: the immature stage of a mushroom

clavate: club-shaped

coniferous: cone-bearing trees and shrubs such as pines, spruces, and firs

conk: a large, woody polypore growing on wood

corrugated: wrinkled, usually with long wavelike ridges

cortina: spiderweb-like partial veil

cuticle: the outermost tissue layer of the cap; skin

decurrent: gills that descend or run down the stalk

deliquesce: liquefy; as in the gills of the genus *Coprinus*

disc: the central area of the surface of a mushroom cap

duff: the partially decayed plant material on the forest floor.

egg: the immature button stage of *Amanitas* and stinkhorns

fairy ring: an arc or circle of gilled mushrooms arising from a mycelium that expands outward from a central point

fibril: a tiny fiber

filiform: thread-like

flesh: the inner tissue of a fruiting body

fluted: having sharp-cornered ridges extending down the stalk

free: gills that are not attached to the stalk

fruiting body: the fleshy to hard reproductive structure of a fungus, commonly called a mushroom

fusiform: spindle-shaped; tapering at both ends

gasteromycetes: a group of basidiomycetes, such as puffballs, which produce spores in closed chambers within the fruiting body

glabrous: smooth

gleba: spore-bearing tissue of stinkhorns

globose: round; globe-like

gregarious: closely scattered over a small area

heartwood: the inner, usually dead wood, of a tree trunk

hirsute: covered with a dense layer of long stiff hairs

humus: partially decomposed plant material

hypha (hyphae): filament- or thread-like cells of a fungus

lamella: a gill on the underside of the cap of a mushroom

latex: a watery or milk-like fluid that exudes from some mushrooms when they are cut or bruised

lignicolous: growing on wood

mycelium: a mass of hyphae, typically hidden in a substrate

mycology: the scientific study of fungi

mycorrhizal: having a mutually beneficial relationship with a tree or other plant

myxomycota: slime molds

ovoid: somewhat egg-shaped

parasite: an organism that obtains its nutrients from a living host

partial veil: a layer of fungal tissue that covers the gills or pores of some immature mushrooms

pedicels: slender stalks

pileus: the cap of the mushroom fruiting body

pyriform: pear-shaped

plasmodium: the vegetative stage of a slime mold

plicate: deeply grooved, sometimes pleated or folded

pores: the open ends of the tubes of a bolete or polypore

pore surface: the undersurface of the cap of a bolete or polypore, where the open ends of the tubes are visible

pubescent: having short, soft, downy hairs

punctate: marked with tiny points, dots or spots

radial: pointed away from a common central point, like the spokes of a wheel

recurved: curved backward or downward

resupinate: lying flat against a substrate

reticulate: covered with a net-like pattern of ridges

rhizomorph: thick, rope-like strands of hyphae growing together as a single organized unit

ring: remnant of a partial veil that remains attached to the stalk after the veil ruptures

saccate: sheath-like or cup-shaped

saprobe: an organism that lives off dead or decaying matter

sapwood: the living, outer layer of a tree trunk

scabers: small, stiff points on the surface of some mushrooms

scabrous: having scabers

scale: an erect, flattened, or recurved projection or torn portion of the cap or stalk surface

sessile: fruiting bodies that lack a stalk.

serrate: jagged or toothed like a saw blade

sexual: pertaining to fertilization involving two compatible cells

spathulate: spoon-shaped

spines: tapered, downward-pointing projections on the undersurface of some mushroom caps

sporangium: a sac-like microscopic structure in which asexual spores are produced

spore: a microscopic reproductive cell with the ability to germinate and form hyphae

spore case: a structure containing the spore mass in gasteromycetes

squamose: having scales

stipe: the stalk or stem that supports a mushroom

striate: having small, more or less parallel lines or furrows

strigose: coated with long, coarse, stiff hairs

sulcate: grooved

subdecurrent: gills extending slightly down the stalk

substrate: organic matter that serves as a food source for a fungal mycelium

superior ring: a ring located on the upper stalk

symbiont: an organism that lives in a mutually beneficial relationship with another organism

terrestrial: growing on the ground

truncate: appearing cut off at the end

umbo: a pointed or rounded elevation a the center of a mushroom cap

universal veil: a layer of fungal tissue that completely encloses immature stages of some mushrooms

veil: a layer of fungal tissue that covers all or part of some immature mushrooms

ventricose: swollen at the middle

verrucose: warty

viscid: sticky or tacky

volva: a typically cup-like sac that remains around the base of a mushroom stalk when the universal veil ruptures

warts: small patches of tissue that remain on the top of a mushroom cap when the universal veil ruptures

INDEX

MAGAZINES/JOURNALS/WEBSITES/CLUBS

Magazines/Journals

Mushroom, the Journal
www.mushroomthejournal.com

Fungi Magazine
www.fungimag.com

McIlvainea
www.namyco.org/publications/mcilvainea/
mcil_journal.html

Mycology Online

Cornell Mushroom Blog
blog.mycology.cornell.edu

Michael Kuo's online ID guide
mushroomexpert.com

Tom Volk's Fungus of the Month
TomVolkFungi.net

George Barron's fungi
www.uoguelph.ca/~gbarron/

Bryce Kendrick's fungi
www.mycolog.com

David Spahr's Mushroom Collecting
mushroom-collecting.com

Mushroom Observer
mushroomobserver.org

MycoKey
mycokey.com

Database of fungal databases
www.cybertruffle.org.uk www.mykoweb.com

New England Mushroom Clubs

Boston Mycological Club
www.bostonmycologicalclub.org

Berkshire Mycological Society
www.bms.iwarp.com

Connecticut Valley Mycological Society
10 Lounsbury Rd.
Trumbull, CT 06611

Connecticut-Westchester Mycological Association
www.comafungi.org

Monadnock Mushroomers Unlimited
PO Box 1796
Keene, NH 03431

Montshire Mycological Club
PO Box 59
Sunapee, NH 03782

New Hampshire Mycological Society
41 Putnam Hill Rd.
Wilton, NH 03086

Vermont Mushroom Club
vermontmushroom.com

Vermont Mycology Club
PO Box 792
Burlington, VT 05402

Maine Mycological Association
www.mushroomthejournal.com/mma/

Northeast Kingdom Mushroom Society
PO Box 277
Albany, VT 05820

NorthEast Mycological Federation
www.nemf.org

North American Mycological Association
www.namyco.org

White Pine Splotch
Lophodermium pinastri

Not finding any fungi? Go to the nearest white pine, investigate the needles lying on the ground, and you'll doubtless find this species. Not much bigger than a pinprick, it dines on dead as well as dying white pine needles, thus reminding us that fungi are one of Nature's most valuable recyclers.

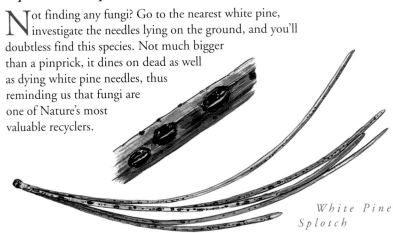

White Pine Splotch